BEYOND KATRINA

The University of Georgia Press

Athens and London

NATASHA TRETHEWEY

Beyond Katrina

A MEDITATION ON THE

MISSISSIPPI GULF COAST

Tenth Anniversary Edition

A SARAH MILLS HODGE FUND PUBLICATION
This publication is made possible in part through a grant from the Hodge Foundation in memory of its founder, Sarah Mills Hodge, who devoted her life to the relief and education of African Americans in Savannah, Georgia.

The poems "Theories of Time and Space" and "Providence" originally appeared in *Native Guard*, by Natasha Trethewey (New York: Houghton Mifflin, 2006). Lyrics from "Backwater Blues" by Bessie Smith © 1927 (Renewed), 1974 Frank Music Corp. All rights reserved. Reprinted by permission of Hal Leonard Corporation.

Tenth anniversary edition published in 2015 by the University of Georgia Press
Athens, Georgia 30602
www.ugapress.org
© 2010 by Natasha Trethewey
Epilogue © 2015 by Natasha Trethewey
All rights reserved
Designed by Mindy Basinger Hill
Set in 11/16 pt Electra LT Std

Most University of Georgia Press titles are
available from popular e-book vendors.

Printed digitally

The Library of Congress has cataloged the original hardcover
edition of this book as follows:
Trethewey, Natasha D., 1966–
  Beyond Katrina : a meditation on the Mississippi Gulf Coast /
Natasha Trethewey.
127 p. : ill. ; 23 cm.
  A collection of essays, poems, and letters, chronicling the effects of
Hurricane Katrina on the Mississippi Gulf Coast.
  ISBN-13: 978-0-8203-3381-6 (hardcover : alk. paper)
  ISBN-10: 0-8203-3381-6 (hardcover : alk. paper)
  1. Trethewey, Natasha D., 1966– — Homes and haunts — Mississippi —
Gulf Coast. 2. Hurricane Katrina, 2005 — Social aspects — Mississippi —
Gulf Coast. 3. Hurricane Katrina, 2005 — Environmental aspects —
Mississippi — Gulf Coast. 4. Hurricane Katrina, 2005 — Economic
aspects — Mississippi — Gulf Coast. 5. African Americans — Mississippi —
Gulf Coast — Social conditions. I. Title.
  PS3570.R433B49 2010
  818'.6—dc22   2010011417

Tenth anniversary edition ISBN: 978-0-8203-4902-2 (paperback : alk. paper)

British Library Cataloging-in-Publication Data available

Opposite page: Natasha and Joe in front of Fort Massachusetts, Ship Island, Mississippi, circa 1999

For Joe

Where you came from is gone. Where you thought you were going to never was there. And where you are is no good unless you can get away from it.

FLANNERY O'CONNOR

Contents

Illustrations

BEYOND KATRINA

Prologue

Years ago, when I began thinking I would write poems, I started recording in my journal the images that had stayed with me — even haunted me — from my childhood. Always in that list were images related to storms: my grandmother's frightened prayers as we moved through the house, rain coming in from the roof; my cousin's nightmare of the ditch around our house spilling a flood into the yard; the annual footage of Hurricane Camille on television; the kerosene lamps we kept atop the tall bookshelf in the den. Still, a long time passed before I realized what the prominence of these images in my notebooks meant. Indeed, they were evidence of the extent to which I, like many people from the Mississippi Gulf Coast, are haunted — even at the edges of consciousness — by the possibility of a natural disaster.

In 1991 I had written those words — *Natural Disaster* — at the top of a page in my journal, recalling a story I had heard as a child about Hurricane Camille. It was a cautionary tale my grandmother likely told me — the story of a rich man who lived by the water and who, despite the potential for loss, embedded a fortune in coins in the floor of his home, a transparent layer above them so that anyone standing in his foyer could see his wealth beneath their feet. In the story, Camille did away with that part of his fortune, and I imagined coins raining down into the Gulf during the hurricane's heavy winds. Later those notes gave way to the poem "Providence," which appears in my 2006 collection, *Native Guard*, and which appears again in these pages, this time serving to underscore the connection between environmental factors and the trajectory of development on the Mississippi coast— both of which are linked to the extent of the devastation wrought— and the lives of the people caught up in this history.

Oddly, not until *after* Katrina did I come to see that the history of one storm, Camille — and the ever-present possibility of others — helped to define my relationship to the place from which I come. And so *Beyond Katrina* begins as that other book began, with a journey home — my *nostos*. "Theories of Time and Space" is the first poem I completed for *Native Guard*. Writing it, nearly ten years ago, I was thinking figuratively, *You can get there from here, though / there's no going home.*

Although I had intended to consider the impossibility of returning to those places we've come from — not because the places are gone or substantially different but because *we* are— by August of 2005, the poem had become quite literal: so much of what I'd known of my home was either gone or forever changed. After Katrina the words I had looked to for their figurative values gave way to the reality they came to represent. For me the poem no longer meant what it had before — even as the words remained the same. In this way, the poem undergoes a kind of revision as it appears here— not unlike the story of the Gulf Coast, which is being revised even now: rebuilding and recovery in the wake of devastation and erasure.

Often I mention this to audiences around the country when I read the poem. But before that, I ask them what they remember when they hear the words *Hurricane Katrina*. Almost all of them say "New Orleans," recalling the footage beginning the day *after* landfall, when the levees broke. Almost never does anyone answer "the Mississippi Gulf Coast."

ONE

2007

Theories of Time and Space

You can get there from here, though
there's no going home.

Everywhere you go will be somewhere
you've never been. Try this:

head south on Mississippi 49, one-
by-one mile markers ticking off

another minute of your life. Follow this
to its natural conclusion — dead end

at the coast, the pier at Gulfport where
riggings of shrimp boats are loose stitches

in a sky threatening rain. Cross over
the man-made beach, 26 miles of sand

dumped on the mangrove swamp — buried
terrain of the past. Bring only

what you must carry — tome of memory,
its random blank pages.

On the dock where you board the boat
for Ship Island, someone will take your picture.

The photograph — who you were —
will be waiting when you return.

Pilgrim

NEARING MY HOMETOWN I turn west onto Interstate 10, the southernmost coast-to-coast highway in the United States. I've driven this road thousands of times, and I know each curve and rise of it as it passes through the northern sections of Biloxi and Gulfport—a course roughly parallel to U.S. Route 90, the beach road, also known as the Jefferson Davis Memorial Highway. It's five o'clock when I cross into Mississippi, and it seems that the sky darkens almost instantly. In minutes it's raining—the vestiges of a storm out in the Gulf—and I can barely see the lights of a few cars out ahead of me. Some are pulled over, parked beneath the underpass. Others slow down but keep going, hazard lights flashing. People have learned to be wary of storms.

"It's different now," my brother, Joe, says. "Before Katrina so many older people told stories of having ridden out Camille that nobody worried much. *That* was the biggest storm to hit around here." Then he recalls the other storm warning, a little while before Katrina hit, and how it turned out to be what he called "a false alarm." "People prepared with supplies," he tells me: "there were long lines at the grocery store and the gas station, but then nothing happened." Emboldened by the "false alarm" and by the fact that her home had withstood Camille thirty-six years before, my grandmother was one of the people who wanted to "ride out the storm" from home. "You remember," he says. "You had to talk her into letting me take her to a shelter."

When I ask her what she remembers, my grandmother conflates the two storms. Ninety-one, a woman who has spent most of her life in the same place, she knows she lives in Atlanta now, where I do, because she had to evacuate after Katrina, but she thinks she was at home during landfall, not lying on a

*Gwendolyn Ann Trethewey née Turnbough and
Natasha, Gulfport, Mississippi, 1966*

cot in a classroom at the public school up the road from her house. Examined by a doctor after evacuating Gulfport, she was disoriented. She hadn't eaten for weeks, even though the shelter provided MREs, even though my brother had been able to drive to Mobile for food. The doctor spoke of *trauma* and *depression*, prescribed medication.

In her room at the nursing home in Atlanta, she recalls how very young I was during Camille and how my parents moved my crib from room to room all night trying to avoid water pouring in through the roof. When I say, "No, Nana — *Katrina*," she looks at me, her eyes glassy with confusion, her lips pressed hard together, her brow deeply furrowed, as she tries to piece together the events of the previous two years. She has layered on the old story of Camille the new story of Katrina. Between the two, there is the suggestion of both a narrative and a metanarrative — the way she both remembers and forgets, the erasures, and how intricately intertwined memory and forgetting always are.

This too is a story about a story — how it will be inscribed on the physical landscape as well as on the landscape of our cultural memory. I wonder at the competing narratives: What will be remembered, what forgotten? What dominant narrative is now emerging? Watching the news, my grandmother turns to me when she sees Senator Trent Lott on the screen. "I made draperies for his house," she says, aware, I think, that theirs is a story intertwined by history: his house gone along with the work of her hands.

I spend the first night catching up with Joe. Because his house and our grandmother's house are still in disrepair, he's living with his girlfriend while doing the work on the properties himself. I've booked a room at one of the hotels on the coast — a casino as most of them are — and we sit in the bar for hours watching the Thursday night traffic on the gaming floor. When the casinos were built on the coast nearly fifteen years before, onshore gambling wasn't permitted. Most casinos then were barges, moored against the beach in the shallow water. One was an old cruise ship, a small one, and it catered mostly to locals. Because of this, even as the state now permits rebuilding on land, a few folks still refer to these new structures as boats. Now and again you'll overhear someone talking about "working on the boat" or "going down to the boat." After Katrina, my brother tells me, the "boats" "couldn't get insurance offshore." This post-Katrina effect and the need to get the economy of the coast rebuilt quickly made the state of Mississippi open the door to rebuilding the casinos on shore. The history of the coast is full of such transformations, and this is not the first time that economic decisions have instigated the overlaying of a new narrative on the Gulf Coast, reinscribing it — transforming it.

In spite of the reservations of many Gulf Coast residents, including nearly half of the residents of Gulfport, the first casino opened on the coast in 1992 after the passage of legislation that approved "dockside" gambling. It wasn't long before the gaming industry made a significant contribution to the coast's economy. Between 1992 and 1996, monthly gaming revenues increased from $10 million to $153 million. Though many casinos transplanted some employees to the coast, creating a larger housing demand and increased traffic problems, most of the people employed in the industry are locals. I can recall both the excitement and the trepidation with which people anticipated the casinos: excitement at the number of new jobs, complete with health insurance and benefits, excitement at the possibility of more entertainment options and of some revenues going to improve local schools. But people also feared an erosion of the coast's cultural heritage, the depletion of wetlands, the transformation of the character of the beach road and surrounding neighborhoods, and a variety of social ills. I watched as title pawn businesses sprang up in the shadows of the newly opened casinos. It was a short walk from the Copa or the Grand in Gulfport to a squat, yellow bunker of a building where you could turn over the title to your car in exchange for a high-interest loan. Often I'd see the same cars parked there for more than a month, and I knew that it meant the owners had missed their pawn deadlines, couldn't "buy" the vehicles back, and that now they would be sold to someone else. Still, the casinos brought an economic boost to the struggling state. Before they opened, the unemployment rate in Mississippi was among the highest in the nation.

In 1992 my brother was nineteen — bored, restless, and hoping for a life in a town with more opportunity, more excitement. After seven years growing up away from his own hometown, Atlanta, he was ready for something more like what he'd left behind or for, at the very least, the abundant opportunity, real or imagined, of a larger city. The casinos brought much of that: steady work in construction and good pay — often untaxed, "under-the-table," he told me back then. In downtown Gulfport a new bar opened — the E.O. Club, which stood for "Early Out" and catered to casino workers getting off their shifts. It was a dark, urban-looking space with a shiny wooden bar, a jukebox by the front door, plants, upholstered chairs, and a stand for the bands playing blues, bluegrass, and covers any given night. Within a few years my brother — good looking, sweet, and effortlessly charming — became a regular. With friends or more likely alone, my brother could talk to anyone. It was how he made contacts in town, found work for himself — and much later, how he would meet people who needed his help in exchange for the construction work they could do.

In this way, Joe is not unlike my great-uncle Son, an entrepreneur who had spent most of his life running a nightclub he owned and buying up rental properties — shotgun houses — in North Gulfport, an area just outside the city limits where blacks had lived for more than a century; where he and his other siblings, including my grandmother, had been born and raised; and where my brother, after the death of our mother, had grown up too. It seemed evident even when we were children that one day Joe would inherit the Dixon family business, that he'd become a landlord like Uncle Son — one who had enough skill to work on the houses, repair them, and who had enough contacts to hire someone else if necessary. It would be years before Joe would decide that this was what he wanted — and years still before a storm would come and change everything.

In 1995, a decade before that storm would hit, the number one reason to visit the coast was the casinos. My brother worked on many of them — including, before its opening in 1999, the Beau Rivage, the most securely moored barge on the Gulf Coast. With some foresight the builders of that casino went beyond the required code of making the structure able to withstand up to 155-mile-per-hour winds, the equivalent of a category 4 hurricane. As a result, the Beau Rivage — with

Willie "Son" Dixon, circa World War II

its fragrant, transplanted magnolias and its hotel views of the water and of the city of Biloxi — suffered much less damage than most of the other casinos. In Gulfport, for example, the Grand Casino — thrust onto land — skidded across Highway 90 and crashed into the church across the street. Secure in its moorings, the Beau Rivage was among the first casinos to reopen in 2006. For employees, this is a blessing.

~~~

The security guard I talk to is a friendly white woman in her sixties, eager, it seems, to talk to yet another visitor with questions about the hurricane and its aftermath. She's been there for ten years, and she's grateful for the job. "Last ones out, first ones in," she says, referring to how long the workers were there trying to evacuate the guests before the storm and to the workers' return. "Lost everything but my job, and when we came back to work, there was hot food from the Salvation Army." There is a mixture of what seems like appreciation for what she does have and a good measure of contempt for the kind of rebuilding taking place. "The casino business is better than ever," she says, "but the people need to have what they used to have." She worries over the practical needs of working people as she describes the developments along the coast: "They say they won't rebuild any gas stations along the beach, just condos we can't afford, and only the casinos can have restaurants. What are the working people supposed to do?"

Her story is not uncommon. After the hurricane her rent increased — despite the terms of her lease, she tells me — from five hundred dollars a month to eight hundred dollars, though her pay did not. When I ask her about assistance from the government, she wags her head fiercely: "Nobody has seen all the money. It's been two years, and we are still suffering. They said they wouldn't price gouge, but they are doing it." In fact, even as the cost of living has risen on the coast, programs dedicated to helping the poor have benefited from only about 10 percent of the federal money, even though the state was required by Congress to spend half of its billions to help low-income citizens recover from the storm. Although state officials, including Governor Haley Barbour, insist that the state does not discriminate by race or income when giving aid to storm victims, many poor residents can't afford homeowner's insurance and thus are ineligible for some aid programs. Renters are altogether excluded from many of them.

When I ask the guard what she remembers of the storm, her face softens as she begins to recall the days after. "It was like a bomb had went off. And now everywhere is slabs, just slabs. And the water is still full of debris — houses, cars. We need to dredge the Gulf to get it all back, including the bodies," she says. "Including the bodies."

It's nearly midnight, and her shift is ending. Beyond the poolside deck where I have been talking to her, the Gulf is flat and black, the lights of the Beau Rivage, reflected on the water, all I can see.

~~~~~~

Walking through the lobby in the morning, I am struck by the incongruousness of the high-end jewelry and clothing stores, the crowds of people bustling with excitement, the countless opportunities for consumption juxtaposed with what I know is just beyond the great entryway with its soaring glass doors, giant flower arrangements, and extravagant perfume. After breakfast in the hotel café, I drive along the beach road, taking note of the few leaves that have begun to fill out the ancient live oak trees anchoring the landscape of the coast. A year ago they were barren, a stark and skeletal imprint against the sky, and I wondered if they would come back. Now the leaves are a green hope above the rubble scattered in the grass. Farther down the beach a pair of them tell a different story of the coast's stark contradictions, its juxtapositions: one with leaves sprouting along its branches, one with none at all.

Compared to the flurry of activity in the casino, downtown Gulfport seems abandoned, empty but for a few new businesses that have opened and a few old ones that have reopened: Hancock bank, a restaurant, a pub, a coffee shop, and Triplett-Day Drugs, which has been there as long as I can remember. At the rusted shell of the former public library a lone light fixture hangs above what was the entry to the stacks. A stairway spirals up to the sagging roof. Vacant lots broadcast one message — AVAILABLE — on sign after sign. Everywhere there are houses still bearing the markings of the officials who checked each dwelling for victims. It's an odd hieroglypics I learn to read — an X with symbols in each quadrant. My brother's girlfriend, Aesha Qawiy, tells me to look for the number at the bottom of the X; it shows how many dead were found. I am relieved each time I pass a house and read a zero there.

When the storm hit, Aesha was living in a lovely apartment atop a law firm just off the Pass Road in Gulfport. A legal secretary at another firm, she'd been a model tenant, paying her considerable rent and saving to buy a house. She was fortunate that the building survived — though with some damage — that some of her things were safe. She and her son sheltered at her parents' house during landfall. Two days later, when she tried to return to her apartment, the owners' daughter was there to evict her. She and her husband needed the apartment, understandably, because their own home had been destroyed. Yet for all the seeming goodwill among people on the coast, the owners' daughter could muster little patience or sympathy for Aesha. Her belongings still inside, Aesha had to search for a storage unit — a good distance away — and when she asked to be given time for an appointment with the FEMA inspector to assess the damage to her personal items, the owners' daughter initially refused, all the while treating Aesha as if this apartment to which she still had a month's claim was something she was stealing. All her clothes and her son's clothes had succumbed to mold and mildew, as had the mattresses and some furniture. She lost items of sentimental value too — sonogram pictures, books. Were it not for her parents, Aesha and her son would have been homeless, and her former landlords didn't care — or couldn't care — so busy were they dealing with their own difficult circumstances.

It would have been quite different if the tenant had nowhere to go and was still being put out of the apartment. No courts were in operation, police were overburdened, and a lawsuit would have been time consuming and perhaps expensive even had the courts been available. Still, Aesha was among the lucky residents of the coast in many ways — her firm reopened quickly, and she had a place to live in the meantime. As she tells her story, it occurs to me that she now marks time by the storms. Like the Gulf Coast Harrison County residents who refer to time before and after Camille as "B.C." and "A.C.," Aesha marks the events of her life as "two days after Katrina" and "the day Rita hit," another hurricane that ravaged the Gulf Coast later that same season.

I think of all this when Aesha and I sit down to talk during my stay. We meet first at a new coffee shop where the young woman behind the counter is cheery and energetic — enthusiasm I take to be a good sign, if not simply the optimism of youth. As we sip tea, I ask Aesha about this optimism, about where she thinks things stand on the coast. She knows this is about something I am writing, and as she answers, I begin to get the feeling that her answers are shaped by her need to govern the narrative of the storm and its aftermath, to control the meaning of the present and the past in the face of an uncertain future. I know she isn't embellishing when she talks about how people interacted after the storm because I've heard these stories from my brother too. "It was as if everyone banded together," she says. "Everyone helped each other. People shared what they had, were even friendlier." I want to remind her of being evicted, of her interactions with the landlord's daughter, but I don't. I know that a preferred narrative is one of the common bond between people in a time of crisis. This is often the way collective, cultural memory works, full of omissions, partial remembering, and purposeful forgetting. People on both sides of a story look better in a version that leaves out certain things. It is another way that rebuilding is also about remembering — that is, not just rebuilding the physical structures and economy of the coast but also rebuilding, revising, the memory of Katrina and its aftermath. In all revisions, words are important. Each time we talk during my visit, another layer of the story of the aftermath and rebuilding is peeled back. Even now, at the coffee shop, Aesha clenches her teeth when she recalls being referred to as a "refugee." "Evacuee," she says. "I am an American — not a refugee in my own country."

The idea of America is inscribed on the landscape of North Gulfport — streets called Jefferson, Madison, Monroe, Florida, Arkansas, Alabama, the names of presidents and states. My cousin Tamara Jones lives just off Highway 49 on Alabama Avenue, at what used to be the intersection of Alabama and Jefferson before Jefferson was blocked off and made a dead-end street. I always thought that change a great irony, as if the very ideals of Jefferson were truncated as the people who lived there became more cut off, more isolated. Even now, thirty years after the street was blocked, ambulances, police cars, and delivery trucks have trouble getting to the houses on Jefferson. On several occasions my brother has had to stand in the street and wave his arms wildly to flag down an emergency vehicle zooming right by us.

Tammy has lived there with her children for nearly two decades. Years ago, when my great-uncle Son died, he bequeathed his house to her. It stands beside the land that once held his famed Owl Club, on the eastern side of Highway 49, easily visible from my grandmother's house on the western side. I pull up in front and park on the crushed shell driveway. Tammy comes out on the porch when she hears my *Yoo-hoo* — the call we've been using all our lives, the call our parents and grandparents used whenever they came to this house.

The porch is stacked with moldy furniture she is intent on reclaiming. Most of it is wooden, except for a few rusted pieces of iron patio furniture. She's been back in the house for a few months, after having lived more than a year in a FEMA trailer on the property while her home was being repaired. It's a sturdy brick house, two bedrooms and one bath on a lot with pecan, fig, and lime trees. Across the street is a similar house. The two houses are mixed in with run-down shotgun shacks and newer prefab homes — all evidence of the working-class and working-poor families in this historically black neighborhood.

I ask her about the rebuilding that has taken place around her since the storm, and she tells a story of generous volunteers. "It was donations," she says. "Donations — and the work of a group from North Carolina — are responsible for most people's repairs in the area. If not for them, I couldn't have completely fixed my house. I'd still be in that trailer." According to the *New York Times*, the state of Mississippi — a couple of years after the storm — had "spent $1.7 billion in federal money on programs that have mostly benefited relatively affluent residents and big businesses." Instead of helping the poor, like most of the residents in Tammy's neighborhood — many who are renters — the money has been used to help utility and insurance companies and middle- and upper-income homeowners. Some houses around Tammy's have been repaired, but many have not. If the owners can't afford to rebuild or repair a badly damaged house, the city demands that it be torn down. "But demolition is expensive," she tells me. "They'll come out and do it for you, tear down what's left of your house and break up the slab and haul it away — but most people out here can't afford what the city charges for demolition." She points to an empty lot beside her house. "If you wait long enough, they'll just tear it down anyway — even if you want to repair your house."

All along the coast, evidence of rebuilding marks the wild, devastated landscape. A little more than a year before, much debris still littered the ground: crumbled buildings, great piles of concrete and rebar twisted into strange shapes, bridges lifting a path to nowhere. Now new condominium developments rise above the shoreline, next to the remains of a gas station, its single overhang, the concrete stripped or gouged, revealing the steel frame, like bones, underneath. Here and there are signs of what's still to come: posters reading "South Beach" and "Beachfront living only better." Other evidence abounds of how slow rebuilding can be. As recently as the second anniversary of the storm, school children in Pass Christian were still attending class in trailers without running water and using portable toilets. Coincidentally, not until *Good Morning America*'s Robin Roberts — a native of Pass Christian — questioned FEMA director David Paulison about the delays did FEMA contract workers begin to dig the new well the school desperately needed. When I spoke to a member of the state House of Representatives from Pass Christian, she complained that the town still hadn't seen the money they'd been promised. "We'd just like a place to buy bread," she said, after introducing herself. "I represent the Pass," she'd said to me, my mind registering, for a moment, the *past*.

Even now whole communities of FEMA trailers line the beach road, the highway, the neighborhoods farther inland — nearly ten thousand of them, many laden with formaldehyde. From a distance they appear as the above-ground tombs of New Orleans' famed cemeteries: white, orderly rows bearing the weight of remembrance. There are concrete steps wedged into the earth leading to nothing. There are concrete slabs so overtaken by grass, roots, and weeds it is as if no one ever lived there — so quickly has nature begun its rebuilding, its wild and green retaking of the land. The devastation reminds me of our fleeting imprint on the landscape, the impermanence of our man-made world, the way nature responds to our folly — our own culpability writ large in the damage wrought by Katrina.

At Jones Park, on the beach across from downtown Gulfport, the picnic area is a muddy plot marked off by orange security netting. The makeshift fence is eerily like the yellow police tape put around locations where a crime or something tragic has occurred. For years this spot had been a place for African American residents of Gulfport to congregate on weekends — families having reunions and cooking out, teenagers and young adults gathering for the rituals of social life in a safe place, out of trouble. I wonder where they are and think of my brother's description of social life now on the coast. "For a long time there was a curfew," he told me. "And after that, there was nowhere to go anyway." To pass time, Joe and his friends drink more than they used to. Even the memory of the work he did for months after — to help with cleanup — haunts the places he encounters daily: how not to look at the sand without that strange anticipation of what might be found there?

Joe comes to visit me in Atlanta as often as possible. I know he wants to spend time with our grandmother, but I know too that he is frustrated with his life on the coast, so he comes to escape, temporarily, that depressed landscape, its reminders of loss at every turn. Flannery O'Connor's words ring true:

Where you came from is gone. . . . Where you are is never any good unless you can get away from it.

~~~~~

Back at the casino for dinner that night, Joe, Aesha, and I sit outside on the patio, taking in the balmy evening air. I am telling them about a man I encountered at lunch — an official casino "host" making his rounds to check on the patrons. The conversation with Bob Short began as many of my conversations do in Gulfport — a quizzical look of semirecognition, then the question *Where are you from?* And then *Who are your people?* Satisfied by my answers, he too was eager to tell me what he thought about life now on the coast.

Before working at the casino as a host, from 1997 until 2001 Bob Short was mayor of Gulfport, and before that he served as a state legislator. His job as a host is to greet patrons of the casino, chat with them, and make them feel at home in a place quite the opposite. Inside, with the whirring of the sirens above the slot machines, the fog of cigarette smoke, the crowds waiting in line for the buffets, it's easy to forget the outside — to forget home — what the owners don't want you to think about even when there isn't the devastation of a storm still marking the landscape. The hotel, the restaurants, the gaming floor are all meant to be an escape from ordinary life. When I ask Bob Short if he thinks the people of the coast can escape the memory of the hurricane, get a reprieve from it, he draws upon his experience as an educator to make this prediction: "Children here are going to have the same posttraumatic stress disorder as Vietnam vets when they get to be twelve or so. One child I know is afraid to take a bath now because he saw his mother washed out of the house by the storm." As I tell the story of my encounter

PJ, *Joe, and Aesha, circa 2003*

with him, Aesha clicks her tongue at this part, thinking, I am sure, about her son and my niece, Joe's daughter PJ, who were extremely clingy and nervous for a long time after Katrina.

When I asked the former mayor about his personal losses, he told me he'd been a collector of sports memorabilia. "It's all gone now," he said. "I can never get back what I had."

The young waiter serving our table has been listening off and on to the story, and he has his ideas too, wants to share them — even gives me his card so that I won't forget his name. He's from Louisiana, and he moved to the coast for restaurant work in the casino. "What's different now is that the new generation respects the hurricanes, unlike the folks before. It needed to happen." When I ask him what he means, he replies vaguely: "to teach us something" and "a cleansing, that's what it was." When he turns to attend to another table, I feel uncomfortable thinking about what he might have meant, particularly after hearing some people opine about New Orleans and who was turned out: the poorer, working classes — overwhelmingly African American — all lumped together with supposed criminals that the city would rather not see return.

In the morning the sky is clear and blue. As I drive along the beach highway, I'm struck by how deceptively beautiful the water looks from a distance. The light makes it seem blue-green, though I know that up close it is a muddy brown and so shallow you have to walk out very far, half a mile perhaps, just to be in waist deep. Beyond that line, what has not been recovered still lurks beneath the surface. I'm still thinking about the idea of "cleansing" when I park in one of the bays and flip through a Fodor's Gulf South tourism guide. There is ominous foreshadowing in the guide that was published, not too long ago, in 2001: "Look on the positive side," it reads. "As long-time residents will remind you, obliging hurricanes will continue to obliterate the latest of mankind's follies."

Those words seem not to anticipate a coast where only "folly" seems to be returning with any ease, where some aspects of the former heritage of the coast are bulldozed and paved over, obscured beneath the concrete slabs of casinos and condominiums. Nor would they seem to coincide with the waiter's notion of cleansing: I imagine the casinos weren't what he wanted to see washed away — but then, I don't know what he meant.

Can the residents of the Mississippi Gulf Coast, caught in the aftermath of Katrina — of recovery and rebuilding — conquer this storm? I posed this question to historian and activist Derrick Evans. Born and raised on the coast, he has returned home to help rebuild Turkey Creek, another historic enclave within North Gulfport. "I don't want to be able to say I can see the future," he told me, "but the devastation of the storm will not surpass the devastation brought on by the recovery."

A *cleansing*, the waiter said. Erasure wrought by wind and water.

Looking west toward Pass Christian, toward Waveland and Bay St. Louis — ground zero for the storm's devastation — I consider the obvious metaphor in this stretch of nearly barren coastline: a slate wiped clean, or nearly clean. Then recovery, rebuilding: another version of the story.

Providence

What's left is footage: the hours before
      Camille, 1969 — hurricane
          parties, palm trees leaning
in the wind,
      fronds blown back,

a woman's hair. Then after:
      the vacant lots,
      boats washed ashore, a swamp

where graves had been. I recall

how we huddled all night in our small house,
      moving between rooms,
          emptying pots filled with rain.

The next day, our house —
      on its cinder blocks — seemed to float

      in the flooded yard: no foundation

beneath us, nothing I could see
      tying us   to the land.
      In the water, our reflection
          trembled,
disappeared
      when I bent to touch it.

Before Katrina

SHIPS ENTERING THE HARBOR at Gulfport, the major cross-roads of the Mississippi coast, arrive at the intersection of the beach road, U.S. 90, and U.S. 49 — the legendary highway of blues songs — by way of a deep channel that cuts through the brackish waters of the Mississippi Sound. Off the coast, ranging from just a half mile to nearly ten miles out, a series of barrier islands — Cat, Horn, Petit Bois, Deer, and Ship, as well as some long-submerged sand keys — bracket the coastline. I cleave to the window as the plane makes a turn over the water and then back inland toward the airport in North Gulfport, trying to see what aerial photographs show — the barrier islands, like a row of uneven stitches, hemming the coast. Some of the islands are invisible from the shore; others loom up in a rise of pine trees against the horizon. Only the legendary Dog Key has completely disappeared, and with it the site of the Gulf Coast's early gaming industry, echoed now in the name of one casino: the Isle of Capri.

It is commonplace that the landscape is inscribed with the traces of things long gone. Everywhere the names of towns, rivers, shopping malls, and subdivisions bear witness to vanished Native American tribes, communities of former slaves, long-ago industrial districts and transit routes. We speak these names often unaware of their history, forgetting how they came to be. Each generation is further from the events and the people to which the names refer — these relics becoming more and more abstract. No longer talismans of memory, the words are monuments nonetheless. As Robert Haas has written, "A word is elegy to the thing it signifies."

The ordinary markers are there — in Gulfport, a neighbor-hood named the Car Line, so called because it was the last stop for the streetcar, the end of the line. Across the railroad tracks that separate the areas closest to the beach and the center of Gulfport from the outlying areas is a community called The Quarters, so named, my grandmother tells me, for all the black residents, as if it were a slave quarters. There is irony in the signifying too: the Isle of Capri, near Point Cadet in Biloxi, was the first casino to open its doors, back in 1992, and it bears a name similar to a pleasure resort and casino that operated just off the Mississippi coast in 1926 — The Isle of Caprice.

A glamorous structure on a raised pavilion, with boardwalks connecting the outlying cabanas to the main house, the resort hovered above the sand on what had been Dog Key. The Isle of Caprice was a popular destination for patrons of the sporting life as well as for families out for a picnic. Visitors from as far away as California and nearby residents from the mainland arrived on boats that left the dock three times a day. They could sunbathe or swim, then listen to big-band orchestras, dance, dine, and gamble in a setting that was opulent with stuffed divans, thick carpets, and mahogany gaming tables.

Aptly named, the resort was a place for whimsy and postwar revelry — a way for pleasure seekers to forget or move on from the past — and a boon for the coast's tourism industry. Built on a sand shoal in an ecosystem characterized by hurricanes, erosion, and shifting landmasses, the resort's name proved to be prophetic as well. After a few years the waters began to overtake the key, never fully receding. By 1932 it was gone, completely submerged, Dog Key retaken by the capricious Gulf waters — a reclamation engineered by the winds and rains of storms.

In 1932 my grandmother, the second youngest of seven children born to Eugenia McGee Dixon and Will Dixon, was sixteen. Her parents had moved to Gulfport around the turn of the century, just two years after construction of the deep-water port and the signing of the town's charter of incorporation by the governor of Mississippi. The first boundary stakes had been driven in 1887, but Gulfport got its second start when multimillionaire oilman Captain Joseph T. Jones bought the struggling Gulf and Ship Island Railroad, continued its construction, and began dredging a deep channel from Ship Island to the end of the car line.

The young couple must have imagined the great possibility of work for Will on the docks in a budding lumber-shipping industry and work for Eugenia as a domestic in the mansions along the beach. The coast's seafood industry, which had been established when the first canning plant opened in the late nineteenth century, didn't employ blacks. Most of the workers were drawn from the influx of Yugoslavs and Slovenians to Biloxi in 1890, as well as other men, women, and children of European descent, many of whom were Polish immigrants brought in from Baltimore and Acadians transported from Louisiana as the industry grew.

Will and Eugenia left the cotton fields of the delta behind them, trading life along the Mississippi River for life on the Gulf Coast. They settled just outside the city limits, acquiring land from a man called Griswold, for whom the community was named. The area, now known as North Gulfport, has been — for as long as my grandmother can remember — a black section of town. It would be several years before the young couple's troubles started, before Will Dixon would leave the

Eugenia McGee Dixon (in center, left arm propped) and her children, left to right: "Son," Hubert, "Sugar," Bertha, Leretta, Roscoe, "Big Sister," and an unknown child outside the original Dixon house on Jefferson Street in North Gulfport, circa 1922

family and never return, years before my grandmother would wake in the middle of the night and see her mother fall back onto the bed from the chamber pot where she'd been sitting, dead — most likely from influenza, a pandemic making its way into port cities around the world. Between 1918 and 1919 — and even into early 1920 — the pandemic swept the Mississippi Gulf Coast leaving at least ten thousand people, on record, dead. Like many forgotten histories, it is one of the narratives of the Gulf Coast that is rarely told.

Gulfport grew a good deal during the childhoods of my grandmother, Leretta, and her siblings — the paving of the roads in 1908, the first hospital in 1909, the library in 1917. In the early 1920s, raising themselves after the death of their mother, the children made money at all sorts of jobs. One brother, Roscoe Dixon, worked at a slaughterhouse and brought home meat. The girls took in wash, cooked, and cleaned houses. All of them crabbed in the Gulf and sold their catch to the white people whose homes fronted the coastline. Though segregated, the narrow, natural beach was open to blacks for the purpose of crossing over to the water to set crab traps and to carry their harvest to the back stoops of those big houses. The only part of the beach my grandmother recalls being designated for blacks was across from Beauvoir, the last home of Jefferson Davis — former president of the Confederacy.

Hubert Dixon, another of Leretta's brothers, worked as a bellhop at the Great Southern Hotel. Captain Jones had built the hotel — a 250-room structure at the end of Twenty-fifth Avenue in Gulfport Harbor — in 1903. A three-story U-shaped building overlooking the water, it operated until its demolition in 1951. Leretta recalls in great detail the stories her brother told of working at the hotel — the excitement on the coast as visitors arrived, all the bustling to and from Union Station. One of the most notorious visitors was Al Capone — there to partake in offshore gambling — who upon arrival shook Hubert's hand. In Leretta's memory, Capone ran a casino out in the Gulf — on Ship Island — ferrying guests out there on a private boat. Ship Island was home only to a rustic fort once manned by black Union troops during the Civil War. More likely, while on the coast, Capone would visit the Isle of Caprice.

The year 1932 brought an end to that: Capone in prison and offshore gambling gone, for a while at least, from the Mississippi Gulf Coast. Much too late had the owner of the Isle of Caprice, Walter Henry Hunt, planned to build a protective seawall. The narrative of legalized offshore gambling had been written — then quickly erased by the Gulf waters. Even as the tourism industry again lagged, the shipbuilding, shipping, and seafood industries, and later the presence of a large military base — as well as revenues from "fines" for illegal backroom gambling — would bolster the coast's economy for years to come. It was in such an atmosphere of growth and possibility that Leretta's oldest brother, Son Dixon, a budding entrepreneur, imagined building a nightclub. He would return from his World War II naval tour of duty with a plan.

The Owl Club stood on two lots of land on Alabama Avenue just outside the city limits in unincorporated North Gulfport. Son Dixon built the low-ceilinged barroom and dancehall next to his own house — a driveway and a garage that held his wife's pink Cadillac separating the two structures. Business

Son Dixon, center right, leaning on the cash register in his Owl Club on Alabama Avenue in North Gulfport in the 1950s

Leretta Dixon Turnbough on the beach,
Gulfport, Mississippi, circa 1940

was good. Every day working men sidled up to the mahogany bar to smoke cigars and drink. The walls were lined with bottles of whiskey and Regal Quarts cans of beer. A jukebox in the corner played records that Son Dixon bought on his monthly trips to New Orleans. Leretta worked for her brother in the kitchen, frying chicken or fish, simmering pots of red beans. Before long, he'd made enough money to start buying property in the area that had been known as Griswold Community.

Stacks of quitclaim deeds in a strongbox in the family safe show Son Dixon's acquisition of large corner lots on major thoroughfares in North Gulfport — the intersections of old Highway 49 and a street now named Martin Luther King Jr. Boulevard; MLK and Alabama Avenue; MLK and Arkansas — and other properties on Florida or backed up to new Highway 49. The dates on the deeds, the calendar from Leretta's beauty shop, the early Eisenhower for President button — who knows why it was saved? — all hint at a story of 1950s Gulfport.

By near midcentury the protective seawall along the Mississippi coast had been built, the government had transformed Highway 90, the coast road, into America's first four-lane superhighway, and plans were underway to create a twenty-six-mile-long sand beach in Harrison County fronting the towns of Gulfport, Biloxi, Long Beach, D'Iberville, and Pass Christian. County officials saw the creation of the sand beach as a way to boost tourism and the postwar economy of the coast. The highway literally paved the way for more urban waterfront development — hotels and restaurants — and began the inscription of several new narratives, cross-written over the landscape.

The "longest man-made beach in the world" was completed

in 1955. The restaurants and hotels alongside it, lit up by neon signs, were for whites only. In a photograph, my grandmother stands on the small part of the beach designated for "colored" people. She is smiling, though it will not be until 1968, four years after the passage of the Civil Rights Act, that the beaches are finally fully integrated. My grandmother remembers going to the lunch counter at the Woolworth's in downtown Gulfport, just a few blocks from the beach, and encountering an elderly white woman and her daughter. "When the woman saw me sit down at the counter," my grandmother tells me, "she asked her daughter to take her somewhere else." The daughter said, "Mama, they're going to be everywhere." "It used to be color," my grandmother muses. "Then the only thing that could keep us out of those restaurants on the beach was money."

Between 1940 and 1950, when Son Dixon began building tiny shotgun houses and duplexes in North Gulfport, Gulfport's population increased by 50 percent. The installation of the beach stimulated the postwar economy in southern Mississippi — the Gulf Coast was again a tourist destination, and Gulfport was growing. People needed places to live, and Son Dixon's properties — which as recently as the early 1990s rented for only two hundred dollars a month — were affordable. The inauguration of Mayor Milton T. Evans in 1949 marked the beginning of the biggest growth period in the history of Gulfport. In fact, the city underwent so much construction that a City Manager's Association survey estimated that it had a higher percentage of new buildings than most other cities with similar population. This too would begin to inscribe a troubling narrative on the landscape of coastal

Mississippi. Opportunities followed growth, but so did environmental havoc.

Shore erosion is a natural occurrence on the Gulf Coast. With rising sea levels, water overtakes land and marshes disappear as nature revises the landscape. Evidence of the loss of wetlands in the United States has been documented since the turn of the twentieth century, and along the Mississippi Gulf Coast significant changes have taken place since the 1950s. Between 1950 and 1992, developed land usage tripled, and nearly 40 percent of marsh loss can be attributed to replacement by developed land — a man-made problem that would have dire consequences. Among the most valuable ecosystems on earth, wetlands are greatly responsible for cleansing polluted water, recharging groundwater, and absorbing storm wave energy. In Gulfport and Biloxi, where dredge-and-fill commercial, industrial, and residential development has been extensive, scientists have recorded high rates of marsh loss. Indeed, it was this man-made problem that rendered the Mississippi Gulf Coast more susceptible to hurricane devastation — the shoreline more vulnerable to the powerful storm waves that battered the landscape along Highway 90.

When Hurricane Camille hit in August 1969, just a year after the beaches were fully integrated, the surge in building and development along the coast that began in 1950 had already reduced the wetlands. With less marshland to absorb storm wave energy, the winds that battered the coast reached a recorded 210 miles per hour, and the storm surge reached more than 25 feet above normal sea level. The length of Harrison

County's beachfront was devastated. More than six thousand residential and commercial buildings were destroyed and many more damaged. The local death count was 132.

Every hurricane season I can remember began with footage of Camille on the news. Always there were the scenes of waves crashing onto the beach, palm trees leaned far enough over to brush the sand with their fronds. And then there were the images of destroyed houses and apartment buildings, a grave voice warning us to evacuate as the camera pans over the devastated site of a hurricane party where the revelers all died in the storm. On the beach in Gulfport, a small tugboat washed ashore. Someone renamed it the *USS Hurricane Camille* and turned it into a souvenir shop — a reminder of the storm, and a place to buy trinkets, the kitschy talismans of memory. It was still standing in the same place after Katrina — all around it destruction, the name of one storm emblazoned on its side in the midst of another: an ironic marker of an event in history to which the children of Katrina and beyond are distanced. It is perhaps as abstract to them as Katrina is real. As I write, though the *USS Hurricane Camille* still stands, the foundation of the Richelieu Apartments — where twenty-three people died during Camille — was bulldozed in 1995. For so long a reminder — a monument to the dead — the site now holds a shopping center.

Son Dixon fared well through Hurricane Camille. His house — made of brick and anchored to a concrete slab rather than perched on cement blocks — suffered only minor roof damage. Even the wooden shotgun houses he owned around North Gulfport were easily repaired with work he could do

himself. Only as he got much older did he begin to hire laborers to do some of the work for him. Then too, at the urging of
his sister Leretta he sold off several of the thirty or so houses
he'd acquired over the years since 1950. When he died in 1992,
the year the first casino opened its doors and several years after
the death of his wife, he left most of the property to Leretta
and her grandchildren. My brother, Joe, was eighteen when he
moved into Son Dixon's garage apartment next to the empty
lot where the Owl Club had been. He was not ready — at least
not yet — to move into his great-uncle's line of work.

Joe recalls his own anticipation of the casinos' arrival on the
coast. On the eve of his twenty-first birthday he counted down
the hours until midnight when he could enter the Grand in
Gulfport for the first time and order a drink. To him, a young
man who'd been born and raised half his life in Atlanta, the
Gulf Coast was a string of sleepy little towns. For most of his
time there, opportunities were limited and there was little to
do. Mississippi had been hit by a severe economic crisis in the
1980s, but in 1990 state legislators drafted the Mississippi Gaming Control Act, which established the provisions for legalized
gaming: first, no gambling was permitted on Mississippi soil but
only on "vessels" docked along a shoreline; and second, these
sites were only allowed along the Mississippi River and the coast
of the Mississippi Sound and only as long as local residents did
not object. Site restrictions limited the locations for the casinos
in the three southernmost counties — Harrison, Hancock, and
Jackson — to the beachfront. Jackson County rejected dockside
gambling, so land speculators searched for spots in the other
two counties — in existing ports, harbors, and marinas, and
in historic urban areas such as downtown Biloxi and Biloxi's

declining seafood district at Point Cadet. That area would soon become known as "Casino Row." The gaming industry had arrived, bringing with it something more for my brother to do.

Between 1992 and 1996 the number of hotel rooms on the coast increased from six thousand to more than nine thousand. There was work in renovating existing hotels and in constructing new ones, and Joe quickly got a job at Treasure Bay — a casino moored in the marina — demolishing and building walls and installing carpet and wallpaper in the old Royal D'Iberville Hotel across the street. He often worked among recent immigrants from Mexico, laborers who were at that time doing more of the unskilled jobs, all of them — including Joe — receiving their pay in cash. Without any health insurance benefits, including workman's compensation, when any of the workers sustained injuries on the job, they paid for the trip to the emergency room themselves.

This kind of work lasted quite a while. Joe purchased his own tools and was frequently called to jobs at hotels along the coast and in other cities, including New Orleans. He'd spend weeks living in whatever hotel he was working on, in whatever city, eating some meals in the hotel restaurant or at fast-food joints. When he grew tired of that kind of food, he bought an electric grill and cooked in the room. At night he and the other men visited the local bars — especially those in the French Quarter. He was young, and this was an exciting life with good pay. He was a hard worker — efficient and likeable — and before long the contractors were seeking him out, often to lead a crew. When construction began on the Beau Rivage, Joe was back on the coast, living in one of the houses he'd inherited years before. And he was steadily gaining experience working at construction sites, doing remodeling — carpet, wallpaper, paint, interior walls, and ceilings — gaining the kind of skills that, along with fixing minor roof problems, switching out appliances, and repairing sinks and toilets, he'd need to have in order to do a good deal of the maintenance on his own rental properties.

In the years leading up to the landfall of Hurricane Katrina, the gaming industry — with its increased opportunities not only in construction work but also in other jobs such as card dealing, security, management, and food service — had a great impact on the lives of Joe and his friends. Some of them went to dealer's school, while others worked as security guards or clerks at cash-out windows. Many of them worked in one casino and socialized next door in another. In many ways, the industry became a lifestyle for some locals, and its influence was significant. In Biloxi, the school system improved as a result of casino revenues, as did the police department: education and public safety — two things that might help to mediate the impact of the industry on social ills. Still, not enough had been done to anticipate the impact on the environment.

Prior to Katrina, the Mississippi Department of Marine Resources documented direct and indirect impacts of dockside gaming on the coast in the form of dredging for barge placement, water-bottom and wetland fill, shoreline alteration, water-bottom shading, increased surface-water runoff in impervious areas, and degraded water quality easily visible in the pollutants washing into coastal waters. By 1998 dead fish and debris were a frequent sight along the beach.

In the year leading up to landfall, a few miles up Highway 49 from the beach, my brother was beginning work on the shotgun houses. The boost in tourism brought by the casinos had created a greater need for housing. North Gulfport had finally been annexed, and the strip of Highway 49 that ran right through it was undergoing a great deal of development. Where there had been darkness for so many years, street lights appeared, guiding travelers from the beach to Interstate 10, past the Wal-Mart, fast-food restaurants, motels, gas stations, and convenience stores, up to the new outlet mall. His property was right in the middle of it, most of it at the crossroads of old Highway 49 and MLK Boulevard. My grandmother was delighted at last to see him take over the family business.

So were people in the neighborhood. Ella Holmes Hinds, city councilwoman for the district, had long been fighting to keep the residential sections of the community intact, not overtaken by the businesses that wanted to acquire the land cheap and transform it into a commercial district. Everywhere there were For Sale signs, signaling that much of the property had already been rezoned for commercial use. For years the shotgun houses Son Dixon built had languished in a state of disrepair — unpainted, sagging — many still occupied by tenants who'd been there since he was alive, the rest vacant or occupied sporadically by drug users. The remaining tenants had paid the rent, now up to $250 a month, steadily for years — Miss Mary in the duplex at the corner of MLK and Arkansas, Chapman's fruit stand and A. D.'s bail-bond business at old Highway 49 and MLK. Armed with tools and experience, Joe began repairing each one, putting in new floors and carpet, new countertops and appliances, brushing on a good coat of paint. Miss Mary nearly cried when Joe fixed up her house. Each day, whenever he was outside, someone would drive by, stop, and roll the window down to look. "People kept coming by to say 'thank you,'" he told me. And, "Man, I appreciate what you're doing for the community." For many longtime residents it must have seemed as if Son Dixon had returned in the form of his young nephew. By the start of the summer of 2005 nearly all of the houses were renovated and rented. In a few months, with a profit, Joe could get them insured.

One of Joe's newest tenants was Clint — white, middle-aged, and recently arrived from Texas with his girlfriend, looking for work. They met one night at a bar after work when Clint was asking about construction jobs in the area, and the bartender suggested he speak to Joe. Because Joe was still occasionally putting together work crews for a contractor and because he had also begun renovation on the house he planned to live in, next to his grandmother's house, he offered Clint a job and a place to stay. Clint would do the work on the house in exchange for rent in one of the last available shotgun houses. With nowhere else to go and no car to get there, Clint and his girlfriend would ride the storm out in the tiny, wooden house. So would Miss Mary in her duplex.

Katrina made landfall on August 29, 2005. Out in the Gulf, Ship Island was completely submerged — the storm surge up to twenty-seven feet. Mississippi officials recorded 238 deaths; tens of thousands of people were displaced. Even though she was a renter, Miss Mary had lived in her duplex for nearly thirty years. She survived the storm in it, but before long she'd have to leave as the severely damaged structure began to fall down around her. Hearing her story, I thought of Bessie Smith's

"Backwater Blues": *When it thunders and lightnings and the wind begins to blow, there's thousands of people ain't got no place to go.* The kind of repairs her house would need Joe couldn't afford to do; he'd spent all his savings on repairing them prior to the storm. Before the second anniversary of landfall, the city would demolish the duplex, and my brother would be struggling to pay the taxes on vacant land.

In the weeks following the storm, Joe busied himself, like a lot of coast residents, aiding the efforts to get food and water to victims. He unloaded trucks, stacked boxes of supplies, handed out diapers and water bottles, clothing and canned goods, to people lined up in the heat. He cleaned out our grandmother's refrigerator filled with mold and spoiled food. He patched what he could of Miss Mary's roof. He waited for rain to take a shower. He sat up in the hot, dark house with his grandmother, listening as she fell asleep; listening to the sirens of police cars passing by; listening for the sounds of anyone not inside for curfew; into the night, just listening.

He got a job directing traffic, standing on the highway waving a flag. He got a job removing debris, clearing the roadways, sorting through the remnants of life before Katrina. He stood in line for a check. He got a job cleaning the beach. He got a job as a watcher, scanning the white and glaring sand for debris that would clog the machines that cleaned the beach. He told me they were looking for chicken bones, scattered there from the warehouses, and for the carcasses of animals. On a quarter tank of gas, he drove to Mobile for supplies. He bought candles and flashlights, food and water, medicine for his grandmother, and beer. He drank with his friends. They drank and looked at the destruction and rubbed their heads and drank some more. He drank on the porch in the evenings by himself. He sat watching the trucks go by on Highway 49. He found a hill where his cell phone worked and called to say, "Everything is gone."

Hegel wrote, "When we turn to survey the past, the first thing we see is nothing but ruins." As I contemplate the development of the coast, looking at old photographs of once new buildings — the pride of a growing city — I see beneath them, as if a palimpsest, the destruction wrought by Katrina. The story of the coast has been a story of urban development driven by economic factors and a much-less-than-needed awareness or consideration of the effects of such development on the environment. It can be seen in all the concrete poured on the coast — impervious to rainwater, a strip of parking lots and landfill. It can be seen in the changing narrative, since 1992, of the landscape of historic buildings into a casino landscape of neon and flashing lights and parking decks.

The past can only be understood in the context of the present, overlapped as they are, one informing the other. The present imagery of the devastated Mississippi Gulf Coast is, of course, what forces me to see the palimpsest of ruin in the "before" photographs, and yet turning to survey the past, I did not expect to find what I did. I was going back to read the narrative I thought was there — one in which gambling and the gaming industry, responsible for so much recent land and economic development on the coast, was a new arrival, not something already ingrained in the culture of the place. I expected a narrative in which the seafood industry had simply been replaced by the gaming industry, not one in which they operated side-by-side in many ways until competition from other places, and perhaps indirect environmental effects of the gaming industry, helped foment the seafood industry's decline. I expected to find a story that would tell me that everything had been fine until 1992, when legalized offshore gambling returned, not that the losses to wetlands because of development had already begun as long ago as 1950 — and had continued. Seeing my own need to believe one narrative, I think again of the words of Flannery O'Connor, *Where you thought you were going to never was there.*

As the plane lifts over North Gulfport, over Turkey Creek, turning to sweep out over the sound before heading north and east to Atlanta, I try to see all the places of my childhood that I am once again leaving, putting them, like the past, behind me — though the scrim of loss hangs before my mind's eye. Bessie Smith's lyrics come back to me again: *I went and stood up on some high old lonesome hill, then looked down on the place I used to live.*

Liturgy

THE MORNING AFTER THE STORM, hundreds of live oaks still stood among the rubble along the coast. They held in their branches a car, a boat, pages torn from books, furniture. Some people who managed to climb out of windows had clung to the oaks for survival as the waters rose. These ancient trees, some as many as five hundred years old, remain as monuments not only to the storm but to something beyond Katrina as well — sentries, standing guard, they witness the history of the coast. Stripped of leaves, haggard, twisted, and leaning, the trees suggest a narrative of survival and resilience. In the years after the storm, as the leaves have begun to return, the trees seem a monument to the very idea of recovery.

Such natural monuments remind us of the presence of the past, our connection to it. Their ongoing presence suggests continuity, a vision into a future still anchored by a would-be neutral object of the past. Man-made monuments tell a different story. Never neutral, they tend to represent the narratives and memories of those citizens with the political power and money to construct them. Everywhere such monuments inscribe a particular narrative on the landscape while — often — at the same time subjugating or erasing others, telling only part of the story. In Auburn, Alabama, a plaque in the center of town, meant to describe how the city was founded, reads simply "After the Indians left . . ." As I write this, determined citizens in Gulfport are working to erect, on Ship Island, some kind of monument to the Louisiana Native Guards — the first officially sanctioned regiment of African American Union soldiers in the Civil War — who were stationed there and to whom no monument exists alongside the monument for Confederate soldiers. According to historian Eric Foner, "Of the hundreds of Civil

War monuments North and South, only a handful depict the 200,000 African Americans who fought for the Union." That's only one example of our nation's collective forgetting. With such erasures commonplace on the landscape, it is no wonder that citizens of the Gulf Coast are concerned with historical memory. And no wonder the struggle for the national memory of New Orleans — and the government's response in the days after the levees broke — is a contentious one.

Political contests over the public memory of historical events undergird the dedication of particular sites, the objects constructed, funds allocated, and the story that is to be told. These contests, rooted in power and money, undergird the direction of rebuilding efforts as well — how the past will be remembered, what narrative will be inscribed by the rebuilding. Many of the people I spoke with on the coast were concerned not only about how the storm and aftermath would be remembered but whether it would be remembered at all. A woman waiting in line at a store worried that people were forgetting the victims on the Mississippi Gulf Coast, what they had endured and endure still. "There's a difference between a natural disaster and the man-made disaster of New Orleans," she said. "Don't forget about us." Though she acknowledged that more attention has been given to New Orleans because of the travesty of the aftermath, her own need to inscribe a narrative into our national memory prevailed. "We have suffered too," she said.

The first monument erected on the coast to remember Katrina and the victims of the storm stands on the town green in Biloxi. Part of the memorial is a clear Plexiglas box filled with found and donated objects — shoes, dolls, a flag, pieces of clothing, a cross, a clock. They suggest the ordinary lives of the people and the kinds of things that can be recovered or regained. Taken another way, they symbolize things lost: childhood, innocence, faith — national or religious — and time. A wall of granite in the shape of a wave replicates the height of the storm surge. Even more telling is the dedication: not for whom but *by* whom the monument was commissioned. A gift donated to the city of Biloxi by ABC's *Extreme Makeover: Home Edition*, the memorial not only remembers the storm and the people but also inscribes on the landscape a narrative of the commercialization of memory. The show, broadcast to millions of viewers, must have garnered millions of dollars in advertising. Even as it commemorates the experiences of the hurricane victims, as well as the seeming generosity of the TV show's producers, the benefits to the network cannot be ignored; people will recall the storm, but they will also recall the network and its programming. Still, the monument is small compared to the giant replica of an electric guitar that looms nearby; across the street from the town green, the new Hard Rock Casino and Resort has opened. When sunlight hits the chrome and bounces off the building, it's the only thing you can see.

Inside, the Hard Rock Casino offers a strange counterpoint to the collection of homely objects in the Plexiglas memorial; the walls are covered with memorabilia — all of it supposedly authentic: shoes of famous rock stars, their clothing, instruments, jewelry. The casino had been set to open just before Katrina hit, and some memorabilia washed away in the storm. A small collection of what has been recovered — muddy and misshapen still, showing the effects of the disaster — reminds us that the casinos have suffered too, that they are like us in their appreciation of loss.

Farther down the beach a different kind of monument anchors the memory of the destruction of Katrina: live oaks that did not survive the storm. Rather than seeing them removed, a local chainsaw artist is transforming the dead trees into sculptures that depict the native species of animals on the coast — pelicans, turtles, dolphins, herons — all shaped to suggest movement and perhaps hope for the coast's environmental future.

The future of the Mississippi Gulf Coast's environment is tied to the stability of the wetlands, the possibility of rising tide levels — due, in part, to global warming rates — and the potential impact of humans and development along the coast. Since Mississippi governor Haley Barbour signed a new law allowing onshore gaming, returning casinos such as the Biloxi Grand, the Island View in Gulfport, and Treasure Bay have reopened on land. In March, Harrah's announced plans to construct Margaritaville Casino and Resort on the shores of Biloxi. Taking the place of a historic neighborhood, the project is expected to cost more than $700 million and is the single largest investment in Mississippi since the hurricane. The huge casino, hotel, and retail complex will claim prime, historic property near the Point Cadet area of Biloxi.

When I ask about the future of development in the area, Aesha tells me about the new FEMA requirements for housing elevation levels. "It makes rebuilding too expensive for many poor people," she says. The new regulations stipulate that homes can only be rebuilt twenty yards back from the road, but many homeowners' lots don't extend that far. "Now," she says, "it's likely that they'll be pushed out." It's not hard to imagine a future for the coast in which their absence in the face of the casinos transforms forever the historic character of the area into a glitzy corporate landscape. With the damage wrought by the storm to the seafood industry, the casinos are now the creators of the dominant economic narrative on the coast. They are visually dominant too.

This is perhaps one of the most apparent changes to the Gulf Coast. My brother imagines a future for the coast that resembles that of a resort and vacation town like Panama City. He says Biloxi will be "a nice city — but it just won't look like the old Biloxi." One of the hardest things Joe thinks the future holds for residents of the Gulf Coast is the cost of living. He has little confidence in the development of affordable housing. Only one person he knows lives in an apartment where the landlord didn't raise the rent by the roughly 70 percent that was commonplace in the months following the storm.

Even as he imagines a "nice city," Joe laments the commercial development of the coast by what he calls "out-of-towners" — corporations with big-business interests in the ports and the gaming industry. "So many landmarks are gone," he says, "replaced by something commercial. Everything seems artificial now, and there are only two local restaurants left on the beach — the rest are casino restaurants." Sitting with him in the bar of the Beau Rivage, I see the evidence of this, sometimes in small ways: a glass of wine I order — and pay more for — comes as a completely different, lesser one when we order a second round. When I say this to the bartender, he shrugs, then opens the bottle to pour me what I asked for. It seems a kind of fake, bait-and-switch culture of the new coast: maybe the bartender thought I wouldn't recognize the difference. Perhaps the notion that drives this idea will undergird the inscription of a new coast narrative. As visitors arrive — not knowing the former culture, the architecture, or the landscape — corporate narratives can prevail, cross-written over the small-town story.

Still, as much as Joe worries about the impact of the decisions of "out-of-towners," he points to the coast's growing diversity — its influx of newcomers — as one of the best outcomes of the rebuilding effort. I can see his point; in a region where the vestiges of racism hang on, played out in debates about "heritage" and the Confederate flag, and where only business leaders vote to do away with a symbol that divides rather than unites coast citizens under one banner, the arrival of newcomers must also signal a new coast, a new Mississippi. In their attempts to gain the patronage of all residents and visitors to the coast, businesses are helping to inscribe a more liberal narrative — at least one in which the only color is money green. Immigrants from Jamaica and Mexico are helping to inscribe a more multiethnic narrative, as did the Vietnamese immigrants of the 1970s and the Slovenian and Yugoslavian immigrants — and others of European and African descent — more than a century before that.

Conversely, the biggest loss to the coast Joe measures is in the displacement of the people. "I've lost a lot of friends," he says, describing a social network — a group of people with whom he gathered after work — that has all but disappeared.

People carry with them the blueprints of memory for a place. It is not uncommon to hear directions given in terms of landmarks that are no longer there: "turn right at the corner where the fruit stand used to be," or "across the street from the lot where Miss Mary used to live." Aesha tells me there are no recognizable landmarks along the coast anymore, and I see this too as I drive down the beach. No way to get your bearings. No way to feel at home, familiar with the land and cityscape. In time, the landmarks of destruction and rebuilding will overlap and intersect the memory of what was there—narrative and metanarrative—the pentimento of the former landscape shown only through the memories of the people who carry it with them. With fewer people in the area who remember the pre-Katrina landscape and culture, there's a much greater chance that it will be forgotten. Too, the memory of such events requires the collective efforts of a people—each citizen contributing to the narrative—so that a fuller version of the story can be told. In that way, one hope we can have for the future, beyond the necessities with which we must concern ourselves—environmentally sound rebuilding, fair and equal recovery—is the continuity of culture and heritage fostered by ongoing change and honest, inclusive remembrance of the past.

Rituals of commemoration serve to unite communities around collective memory, and at the second anniversary of the storm people gathered to remember—some at church or community centers, others at locations that held more private significance. Personal recollections are equally integral to the larger story. Johnny, a card dealer at one of the casinos—a friend of my brother's who did not leave—says that he stayed home to watch the national news. He wanted to see how the anniversary and the recovery were being understood outside the region. Then he took a kind of memorial drive—"just riding down the beach," he said, "trying to find places I used to go."

Aesha marked the anniversary by donating blood. When I ask them both about what they do year round to keep the memory of the storm and its aftermath and about whether there is a danger in forgetting, Johnny takes the diplomatic approach: "You have to learn from history," he says. Shaking her head, Aesha is more adamant about the memory of the storm. "There is no forgetting," she says. "You can't forget — you won't." In her words, an imperative, a command.

Some time ago — before the storm — my grandmother and I were shopping in Gulfport, and we met a friend of hers shopping with her granddaughter too. The woman introduced the girl to us by her nickname, then quickly added the child's given name. My grandmother, a proud woman — not to be outdone — replied, "Well, Tasha's name is really *Nostalgia*," drawing the syllables out to make the name seem more exotic. I was embarrassed and immediately corrected her — not anticipating that the guilt I'd feel later could be worse than my initial chagrin. Perhaps she was trying to say Natalya, the formal version, in Russian, to which Natasha is the diminutive. At both names' Latin root: the idea of nativity, of the birthday of Christ. They share a prefix with words like *natal*, *national*, and *native*. "I write what is given me to write," Phil Levine has said. I've been given to thinking that it's my national duty, my native duty, to keep the memory of my Gulf Coast as talisman against the uncertain future. But my grandmother's misnomer is compelling too; she was onto something when she called me out with it.

I think of Hegel again: "When we turn to survey the past,

the first thing we see is nothing but ruins." The *first* thing we see. The fears for the future, expressed by the people I spoke with on the coast, are driven by the very real landscape of ruin and by environmental and economic realities associated with development, but they are driven by nostalgia too. When we begin to imagine a future in which the places of our past no longer exist, we see *ruin*. Perhaps this is nowhere more evident than in my own relationship to the memory of my home.

Everywhere I go during my journey, I feel the urge to weep not only for the residents of the coast but also for my former self: the destroyed public library is *me* as a girl, sitting on the floor, reading between the stacks; empty, debris-strewn downtown Gulfport is *me* at the Woolworth's lunch counter — early 1970s — with my grandmother; is *me* listening to the sounds of shoes striking the polished tile floor of Hancock Bank, holding my grandmother's hand, waiting for candy from the teller behind her wicket; *me* riding the elevator of the J. M. Salloum Building — the same elevator my grandmother operated in the thirties; *me* waiting in line at the Rialto movie theater — gone for more years now than I can remember — where my mother also stood in line, at the back door, for the peanut gallery, the black section where my grandmother, still a girl, went on days designated *colored only*, clutching the coins she earned selling crabs; is *me* staring at my reflection in the glass at J. C. Penney's as my mother calls, again and again, my name. I hear it distantly, as through water or buffeted by wind: *Nostalgia*.

Names are talismans of memory too — *Katrina, Camille*. Perhaps this is why we name our storms.

When Camille hit in 1969, I was three years old. Across the street from my grandmother's house, the storm tore the roof off the Mount Olive Baptist Church. A religious woman, my grandmother believed the Lord had spared her home — a former shotgun to which more rooms had been added — and damaged, instead, the large red-brick church and many of the things inside, thus compelling her to more devotion. During renovation the church got a new interior: deep red carpet and red velvet draperies for the baptismal font — made by my grandmother, her liturgy to God's House. In went a new organ and a marble altar bearing the words *Do This In Remembrance Of Me*. As a child I was frightened by these words, the object — a long rectangle, like a casket — upon which they were inscribed; I believed quite literally that the marble box held a body. Such is the power of monumental objects to hold within them the weight of remembrance.

And yet I spent so little time in the church when I was growing up that I'm surprised now that so much of my thinking comes to me in the language of ceremony. But then, when I look up the word *liturgy*, I find that in the original Greek it meant, simply, *one's public duty, service to the state undertaken by a citizen.*

I am not a religious woman. This is my liturgy to the Mississippi Gulf Coast:

Liturgy

To the security guard staring at the Gulf
thinking of bodies washed away from the coast,
    plugging her ears
against the bells and sirens — sound of alarm —
    the gaming floor
on the coast;

To Billy Scarpetta, waiting tables on the coast,
    staring at the Gulf
thinking of water rising, thinking of New Orleans,
    thinking of cleansing
the coast;

To the woman dreaming of returning to the coast,
    thinking of water rising,
her daughter's grave, my mother's grave — underwater —
    on the coast;

To Miss Mary, somewhere;

To the displaced, living in trailers along the coast,
    beside the highway,
in vacant lots and open fields; to everyone who stayed
    on the coast,
who came back — or cannot — to the coast;

To those who died on the coast.

This is a memory of the coast: to each his own
recollections, her reclamations, their
restorations, the return of the coast.

This is a time capsule for the coast: words of the people
— *don't forget us* —
the sound of wind, waves, the silence of graves,
the muffled voice of history, bulldozed and buried
under sand poured on the eroding coast,
the concrete slabs of rebuilding the coast.

This is a love letter to the Gulf Coast, a praise song, a dirge,
invocation and benediction, a requiem for the Gulf Coast.

This cannot rebuild the coast; it is an indictment,
    a complaint,
my *logos* — argument and discourse — with the coast.

This is my *nostos* — my pilgrimage to the coast, my memory,
    my reckoning —

native daughter: I am the Gulf Coast.

~~~~

Nine months after Katrina, I went home for the first time. Driving down Highway 49, after passing my grandmother's house,
I went straight to the cemetery where my mother is buried.
It was more ragged than usual — the sandy plots overgrown
with weeds. The fence around it was still up, so I counted the
entrances until I reached the fourth one, which opened onto

the gravel road where I knew I'd find her. I searched first for the large, misshapen shrub that had always shown me to her grave, and found it gone. My own negligence had revisited me, and I stood there foolishly, a woman who'd never erected a monument on her mother's grave. I walked in circles, stooping to push back grass and weeds until I found the concrete border that marked the plots of my ancestors. It was nearly overtaken, nearly sunken beneath the dirt and grass. How foolish of me to think of monuments and memory, of inscribing the land-scape with narratives of remembrance, as I stood looking at my mother's near-vanished grave in the post-Katrina landscape to which I'd brought my heavy bag of nostalgia. I see now that remembrance is an individual duty as well — a duty native to us as citizens, as daughters and sons. Private liturgy: I vow to put a stone here, emblazoned with her name.

Not far from the cemetery, I wandered the vacant lot where a church had been. Debris still littered the grass. Everywhere, there were pages torn from hymnals, Bibles, psalms pressed into the grass as if they were cemented there. I bent close, trying to read one; to someone driving by along the beach, I must have looked like a woman praying.

2009

Congregation

Believe the report of the Lord;
Face the things that confront you.

MARQUEE (FRONT AND BACK),
GREATER MT. REST BAPTIST CHURCH,
GULFPORT, MISSISSIPPI, MAY 2009

1. *Witness*

Here is North Gulfport —
its liquor stores and car washes,
trailers and shotgun shacks
propped at the road's edge;
its brick houses hunkered
against the weather, anchored
to neat, clipped yards;
its streets named for states
and presidents — each corner
a crossroads of memory,
marked with a white obelisk;
its phalanx of church houses —
a congregation of bunkers
and masonry brick, chorus
of marquees: *God is not*
the author of fear; Without faith
we is victims; Sooner or later
everybody comes by here.

2. Watcher

AFTER KATRINA, 2005

At first, there was nothing to do but watch.
For days, before the trucks arrived, before the work
of cleanup, my brother sat on the stoop and watched.

He watched the ambulances speed by, the police cars;
watched for the looters who'd come each day
to siphon gas from the car, take away the generator,

the air conditioner, whatever there was to be had.
He watched his phone for a signal, watched the sky
for signs of a storm, for rain so he could wash.

At the church, handing out diapers and water,
he watched the people line up, watched their faces
as they watched his. And when at last there was work,

he got a job, on the beach, as a *watcher*.
Behind safety goggles, he watched the sand for bones,
searched for debris that clogged the great machines.

Riding the prow of the cleaners, or walking ahead,
he watched for carcasses — chickens mostly, maybe
some cats or dogs. No one said *remains*. No one

had to. It was a kind of faith, that watching:
my brother trained his eyes to bear
the sharp erasure of sand and glass, prayed

there'd be nothing more to see.

3. *Believer*

FOR TAMARA JONES

The house is in need of repair, but is —
for now, she says — still hers. After the storm,
she laid hands on what she could reclaim:
the iron table and chairs etched with rust,
the dresser laced with mold. Four years gone,
she's still rebuilding the shed out back
and sorting through boxes in the kitchen —
a lifetime of bills and receipts, deeds
and warranties, notices spread on the table,
a barrage of red ink: PAST DUE. Now,
the house is a museum of everything

she can't let go: a pile of photographs —
fused and peeling — water stains blurring
the handwritten names of people she can't recall;
a drawer crowded with funeral programs
and church fans, rubber bands and paper sleeves
for pennies, nickels, and dimes. What stops me
is the stack of tithing envelopes. Reading my face,
she must know I can't see why — even now —
she tithes, why she keeps giving to the church.
First seek the kingdom of God, she tells me,
and the rest will follow — says it twice

as if to make a talisman of her words.

4. Kin

FOR ROY LEE JEFFERSON

He has the surname that suggests
a contested kinship: *Jefferson* —
the name, too, of this dead-end street
cut in half by Highway 49. Here,
at the corner where it crosses Alabama,
he's perched on the stoop, early evening,
at my cousin Tammy's house, empty
bottles at his feet. When he sees me
opening the gate, walking up smiling,
he reads me first as *white woman*, then —
he says — *half-breed*. It's my hair, he tells me:
No black woman got hair like that,
and my car, a sedan he insists
the cops don't let black people drive,
not here, not without pulling them over
again and again. He's still wearing
his work uniform — grass stains and clippings
from the mower he pushed all day —
and his name tag, a badge, still pinned
to his collar. He tells me he'd swap the badge
for one from another boss, switch jobs
if he could get more pay; says
his boss has plenty of money: *cheese,*
he calls it — *Man's tight with it, he squeak*
when he walk. So Roy waits, biding
his time, he says, *till the Lord bless me*
with something else. When he goes quiet,

I ask him the easy question — one I know
he's been asked a hundred times —
just to hear him talk: *Where were you*
during the storm? That's when he tells me
what he hasn't this whole time, holding it back
maybe, saving it for the right moment:
I got a baby with your cousin Tammy's sister —
that makes us kin. You can't run
from the Lord. I don't know what he sees
in my face, but he grins at me, nodding.
White girl, he says. *You gone come*
see my baby, come up to the country
where we stay? He's walking away now,
a tall-boy in his hand. I'm trying to say,
yes, one day, sure, but he's nearly gone,
looking back over his shoulder, shaking
his head, laughing now as he says this:
When you waiting on kinfolks,
you be waiting forever.

5. *Exegesis*

On Saturday, when I come to see
my brother, they call him over loudspeaker
to the *tower* — a small guardroom
at the entrance to the prison. I sign my name
in the book, write R0470 — his number —
and agree to a search. I stand as if
I would make a snow angel in the air,
and the woman guard pats me down
lightly. Waiting for him, I consider

the squat room's title: how it once meant
prison, and to the religious faithful, *heaven*.
Here, my brother has no use for these words,
this easy parsing. This time he tells me
he's changed his name: Jo-ell instead of Joel —
name of the man who took our mother's life,
his father, an inmate somewhere else.
Thinking only of words, I'd wanted to tell him
the name means *prophet*. That was before I knew

it had — for him — been a prison, too.

6. *Prodigal*

I.

Once, I was a daughter of this place:
daughter of Gwen, granddaughter
of Leretta, great of Eugenia McGee.

I was baptized in the church
my great-aunt founded, behind
the drapes my grandmother sewed.

As a child, I dozed in the pews
and woke to chant the *Lord's Prayer* —
mouthing the lines I did not learn.

Still a girl, I put down the red flower
and wore a white bloom pinned to my chest —
the mark of loss: a motherless child. All

the elders knew who I was, recalled me
each time I came home and spoke
my ancestors' names — Sugar, Son Dixon —

a native tongue. What is home but a cradle
of the past? Too long gone, I've found
my key in the lock of the old house

will not turn — a narrative of rust;
and everywhere the lacunae of vacant lots,
For Sale signs, a notice reading *Condemned*.

*Leretta Dixon Turnbough
and daughter Gwendolyn Ann
Turnbough, circa 1945*

*Frances Dixon Ingram
(Aunt Sugar), circa 1945*

II.

I wanted to say I have come home
to bear witness, to read the sign
emblazoned on the church marquee —
Believe the report of the Lord —
and trust that this is noble work, that
which must be done. I wanted to say *I see*,
not *I watch*. I wanted my seeing to be
a sanctuary, but what I saw was this:
in my rearview mirror, the marquee's
other side — *Face the things that confront you.*

My first day back, a pilgrim, I traveled
the old neighborhood, windows up,
steering the car down streets I hadn't seen
in years. It was Sunday. At the rebuilt church
across from my grandmother's house,
I stepped into the vestibule and found
not a solid wall as years before but
a new wall, glass through which I could see
the sanctuary. And so, I did not go in;
I stood there, my face against the glass,

watching. I could barely hear the organ,
the hymn they sang, but when the congregation rose,
filing out of the pews, I knew it was the call
to altar. And still, I did not enter. Outside,
as I'd lingered at the car, a man had said
You got to come in. You can't miss the word.
I got as far as the vestibule — neither in,
nor out. The service went on. I did nothing
but watch, my face against the glass — until
someone turned, looked back: saw me.   81

High Rollers

Natasha and Joe, circa 1976

SOMEWHERE IN THE POST-KATRINA DAMAGE and disarray of my grandmother's house is a photograph of Joe and me — our arms around each other's shoulders. We are at a long-gone nightclub in Gulfport, The Terrace Lounge, standing before the photographer's airbrushed scrim — a border of dice and playing cards around us. Just above our heads the words *High Rollers*, in cursive, embellished — if I am remembering this right — with tiny starbursts. It is 1992, the year the first casino arrived on the Mississippi Gulf Coast and, with it, a new language meant to invoke images of high-stakes players in exclusive poker games, luxurious suites on the penthouse floor, valet parking and expensive cars lined up in a glorious display of excess. Scenes from a glamorous casino someplace like Monte Carlo or Las Vegas — nothing like the gravel parking lot outside the club, the empty lot beyond it, and the small, run-down houses on either side, each with a chained-up dog barking into the night.

Not far from the club, beyond the spot that held the old Gulfport City Limits sign, is the neighborhood my ancestors settled in when they arrived on the Gulf Coast. Roughly five miles from the beach and downtown, the place called North Gulfport was once the northernmost settlement beyond the city. Now, it occupies a middle ground in Gulfport, though — until just recently — the city of Gulfport's annexation of outlying districts had skipped the entire area to incorporate the white and affluent residential neighborhoods that had developed, due north, beyond it. One of two historically African American communities that sprang up along the Mississippi Gulf Coast after emancipation, North Gulfport has always been a place where residents have had fewer civic resources than those extended to other outlying communities. Isolated and unincorporated, North Gulfport lacked a basic infrastructure: flooding and contaminated drinking water were frequent problems. Although finally incorporated in 1994 — not long after the arrival of the first casino — many of North Gulfport's streets still lack curbs, sidewalks, and gutters. Before the arrival of the casinos brought tourists down Highway 49 toward the beach, there were few streetlights and North Gulfport was cast in darkness. In recent years, as developers have acquired land in the community for commercial purposes — as the city has redistricted homesteads as commercial rather than residential property — many elderly citizens have lost their homes. Higher property taxes have forced people out even as property values have declined. For Sale signs abound, and developers seeking to fill in the nearby wetlands continue to threaten the environmental safety of North Gulfport's residents. Highway 49, rerouted and expanded after World War II, long ago cut the community in half. According to an article published in the July/August 2005 issue of the National Housing Institute's *Shelterforce* magazine, in a state as poor as Mississippi, residents in North Gulfport face "even higher rates of poverty, land loss and housing abandonment than the state average."

When I was growing up there, North Gulfport was referred to as "Little Vietnam" because of the perception of crime and depravity within its borders — as if its denizens were simply a congregation of the downtrodden. Even now, it is a place that outsiders assume to be dangerous or insignificant — run-down and low income, a stark contrast to the glittering landscape of the post-Katrina beachfront with its bright lights and neon bouncing off the casinos onto the water. Were North Gulfport not along the main thoroughfare, making it necessary to drive through to get to the beach, it might be easily forgotten. Now, because the city is invested in improving that stretch of Highway 49, some residents face losing the right to make decisions about their own property. This problem is foremost in Cicero Tims's concerns about the post-Katrina political landscape.

Across Highway 49 from my grandmother's house and down the street from Tammy's, Mr. Tims still runs the business he started years ago — Tims's Snowballs — a little stand that serves as a gathering spot for a lot of people in the community. I haven't seen him in years, but when I stop in, he gives me a free snowball, and we stand in the shade of a big live oak, reminiscing. A longtime friend of my grandmother and my great-uncle, Son Dixon, Mr. Tims has seen a good deal of change around here — and a lot of his stories include my family. In between telling me about what's going on now, he interjects recollections of the past, revealing his thoughts on what he considers to be the two worst things to have happened to this place — one man-made, one natural:

"I've had to start over several times in my life when everything I had was destroyed. This time, the city won't let me rebuild my business the way I want to. This old shack that my snowball stand is in — I can't even tear it down to build a new one. If I tear it down, the city takes the land. I'm only here now because of the grandfather clause. If your business was here before a certain date, you can keep your property. But if you tear it down to do something else, it's gone.

"I've been out here a long time. I remember when your uncle built his nightclub right over there. He was one of only three people out here who had a Cadillac. Owned the ball team too. A high roller — he bought Lizzie that pink Cadillac. I owned a motel back then, and all the colored acts had to stay in it. Son Dixon booked them at his club, and they stayed with me. I did a good business — until they desegregated the white hotels. Before Katrina, the worst thing that happened was desegregation. I lost all my business. Had to shut down the motel. You know where it was — back over there, off old Highway 49."

I'm stunned at first that he has fond memories of a segregated Gulfport, but then I realize that he's speaking figuratively, and I can see the comparison he's making. He's a man who is proud to have put all his children through college — at integrated institutions. Yet his nostalgia about the days of Jim Crow implies that the alternative hasn't always benefited poor and low-income people equally and that reforms that should help all members of a society still privilege some people over others. Rather than simplifying the idea that desegregation was immediately and equally good for everyone, he focuses on the nuances of what some people lost: how suddenly owners of white hotels were able to benefit from the revenues brought in by black consumers at the same time black business owners were losing those customers. Whatever economic base the community might have had because of local businesses began to evaporate when they could no longer afford to stay open. And without a good tax base, the community would receive fewer resources from the city. In his nostalgia for a past in which he had a viable business, he underscores the ongoing discrepancies that have plagued the rebuilding effort on the Gulf Coast.

Turning to scan a blighted radius of North Gulfport that

stretches from one side of Highway 49 to the other, Mr. Tims grows quiet. "What are you going to do with all that property your Uncle Son left?" he asks. Then he points to the vacant corner where several of my brother's rental houses have been torn down, the last one standing with a *Condemned* sign on the front door. "That's some valuable land," he says.

A post-Katrina progress report and housing study published by the Mississippi governor's office for the most recent anniversary reveals that of the 52,512 severely damaged housing units, most of which are located south of I-10, roughly 20 percent have been designated *blight* — vacant lots, lots with only slabs remaining, or damaged structures. Surveying North Gulfport — even from the highway — it appears that a lot of that blight is concentrated here. In an editorial published after the fourth anniversary of the storm, the *New York Times* reported on how much federal aid — assistance that should have gone to poor and lower-income residents — was used, instead, for other projects. Instead of replacing all of the low-income housing lost in the storm, the state of Mississippi found ways to divert those funds for such things as the refurbishment and expansion of the Port of Gulfport — a project that was in the planning stages long before Katrina hit. The editorial, titled "Mississippi's Failure," is certain to anger some coast residents concerned with a kind of historical memory uncritical of the state's version of recovery. In another postanniversary article from the local South Mississippi *Sun-Herald*, the editor — noting that the Mississippi Gulf Coast has been rendered "invisible" by all the coverage devoted to New Orleans — calls for the coast's story to be told. But the version the editor wants to tell — like many residents who responded to the article online — is the triumphant narrative of "the poor little state" that cleaned up, rebuilt, and succeeded in ways that Louisiana failed. This story, with its little-engine-that-could nostalgia, ignores the ongoing experiences of so many poor people whose lives have yet to be rebuilt. And with its "us" and "them" language, the comments also hint at the racial tensions implicit in this difficult story.

One of those tensions was inherent in the strange reopening ceremony at Beauvoir, Jefferson Davis's last home, located on the beach in Biloxi. Anna Harris, curator at the Ohr-O'Keefe Museum of Art, was there for the dedication. When I asked about her perception of rebuilding and historical memory on the coast, she described watching in disbelief as local politicians toasted and pledged allegiance to the Confederate States of America — "even as they had used federal funds," she said, to help rebuild the historic landmark. "I tried to get someone at the newspaper to report on that fact," she told me, "but no one would." Hearing that, I couldn't help worrying about the rebuilding narrative that was emerging and what was being left out or forgotten. Only a few years before, citizens on the Gulf Coast had been embattled in a bitter dispute about the Confederate flag. Back then business leaders had supported removing it from the flagpole between Gulfport and Biloxi to attract investors to the coast.

After my initial journeys back home, following Katrina, I stayed away for a long time, though my grandmother asked again and again to make the trip. *I know I can't live there anymore,* she'd say. *I just want to see it one more time.* For three years I kept putting her off — saying *one day* — so that, at ninety-two, she could at least hold onto the hope of getting there. I never considered the consequences of this tactic, how it might haunt me later. When I started going back more often, it was because I had to, and by then it was too late. It occurs to me now that I had been waiting, foolishly, for the recovery to be complete. I had wanted to show her the place she'd spent her life without the narrative of destruction still inscribed on the landscape.

During the year or so after the storm, everything that had been disrupted seemed to be starting to settle, the narrative of recovery overwriting the devastation. My grandmother had lost a lot of weight during her ordeal, but in the nursing home in Atlanta, she started eating again. My brother too seemed to be on his way to remaking his life. Even without his rental units, he was earning a living; there was a good deal of work to be had on the coast. Government contractors were hiring crews for the work of cleanup — flagging and directing traffic, distributing supplies, scanning the beach for hazardous debris — and Joe was doing it all. I remember too that he called one day, excited about the possibility of a small business loan to rebuild his rental units, though later he'd learn that he did not qualify for assistance. Like a lot of people in North Gulfport, he wasn't eligible for the kinds of programs that had helped businesses and wealthier citizens get back on their feet, and it wasn't long before the initial "cleanup" was done — though "recovery" was still a long way off and still hasn't occurred for some of the poorest citizens in the region. Just more than a year after landfall, the contractors pulled out of Gulfport and other devastated Mississippi coastal towns, leaving behind much less work for people struggling to recover and rebuild their lives. Even the retail store Joe had worked in part-time before the storm did not rebuild on the coast. The owners relocated the business farther north, where they had family. Not only were jobs leaving the coast, much low-income housing had disappeared too and wasn't being rebuilt in the same numbers as before the storm, thus rendering recovery a lot harder to achieve for many citizens.

In the midst of all that devastation and loss — in the spring of 2007, nearly two years after landfall — with no money left from all the work he'd done on the houses before the storm, with taxes due on the vacant land and no buyers for the property, Joe made a desperate decision. When someone he'd known a long time asked him to transport and deliver several ounces of cocaine, he did. He made four thousand dollars. So he did it again. There was still the possibility of a life he imagined — prosperous, stable, perhaps even emotionally rewarding, as it had been when he was first renovating those houses. And it must have been in sight, reflected in the images of the "good life" plastered on casino billboards up and down Interstate 10 and down Highway 49 toward the beach: attractive people, in elegant clothes, laughing into cocktail glasses poised above plates of beautiful, abundant food. The casinos were among the first to rebuild and recover, and they broadcast their message of affluence above the heads of people struggling to reconstruct their lives from remnants.

I can't help thinking too that the photograph we made in 1992 foreshadowed something else. Driving through the old neighborhood not long ago, I remembered that my brother and I had waited in line to have it taken. The line had stretched around the dance floor, and we stood there with everyone else that night to pay the five dollars to pose beneath those words — *High Rollers*. It was as if we needed to get close to that image of luck and money in a place where so many people had so little. Perhaps it's better the photograph is lost. I know the desire to see the images of the past in light of the present would be too strong, and I'd be tempted to read into it — in our gestures, the way we held onto each other — what I would not see then: the irony of those words, the way they mocked so many of the people who had stood beneath them.

Cycle

THE FIRST LETTER MY BROTHER WRITES me during his incarceration arrives on August 13, 2008 — a week after we bury our grandmother. It comes bearing his name and his inmate number, R0470, along with a warning, stamped in red, that the letter is from an inmate and that the facility — the county jail where he awaits sentencing — is NOT RESPONSIBLE FOR CONTENT. He is as stoic in the letter as he was at the church the day of our grandmother's memorial service — *I know things are hard right now. It seems like everything comes at one time* — and I relive that morning while thinking of him trying to be strong in his cell. Perhaps because so much has happened in what seems like a short amount of time, I feel that I have gone through it as if I were walking through a set, an artificial backdrop onto which our lives have been projected along with a story that is already in process and beyond our control. I think of it now as not unlike the fake town at a dude ranch I visited when I was a child. The buildings were run-down, mostly facades, and I was surprised the first time I saw the actors stage a shoot-out. My grandmother and I stood watching, at once part of the scene, because we were there, and not — as though we had walked into some bizarre turn of our lives and it was playing out right there before us, and we were unable to stop it.

The morning we buried our grandmother, the church was like that. Still in disrepair — the sanctuary unused — the church seemed abandoned. On the ground level, windows on both sides of the church were boarded up, and a couple of the high windows up top that overlooked the balcony were still blown out. I could see birds flying in and out of them. The church marquis hadn't been repaired, and most of the glass was missing. A few letters hung on — an O on its side, what looked to be a broken F. Missing it's smaller arm, it resembled the gallows in a child's game of hangman.

Only the small bunker attached to the back of the church was functional. It was the place food was served after services, and it held Sunday school classrooms and a nursery. When I called to tell the caretaker, Mr. Lloyd Croutch, that I was bringing my grandmother's body back to Gulfport to have her home-going ceremony in the church she'd belonged to her whole life, he thanked me. "Since the storm we've lost a lot of our members," he said. "Mount Olive is still struggling to raise the money for repairs that the insurance company didn't cover. Most people have moved on to places that aren't still in the process of rebuilding."

I could understand the difficulties the church was facing. With fewer congregants, the church would take in a lot less in tithes, and the money needed in the budget just to operate — to keep the lights and gas on, even to pay the pastor — wouldn't be there. Mr. Croutch, now in his early eighties, had done this job most of his life, and I wondered if he was being compensated for his work. I had arranged with him to have the doors opened early so that Joe would be able to have some time with our grandmother. The sheriff had granted him permission to come — but only to a private viewing — and we had to schedule it two hours before anyone was supposed to arrive for the ceremony. My husband, Brett, and I arrived early — even before 8:00 a.m., when officers were scheduled to pick him up for transport. We didn't find anyone there when we arrived, no police car, so we decided to circle the block around the building in case they parked somewhere else.

Turning the corner off Jefferson, right in front of my grand-mother's house, onto the access road that runs parallel to Highway 49, we saw them. They were near the intersection of 49 and MLK, headed in the direction of the jail. I could see my brother's head just above the top of the back seat. When I saw the car's blinker come on, I panicked. It seems funny to me now that in moments like this it becomes so easy to ignore the rules of traffic, of law and order on the road. I asked Brett to speed up, and he did, flashing the headlights and honking the horn as he pulled up close behind the police car. When they stopped, I got out of the car and hurried toward the driver.

Later my brother would tell me that the two officers had been skeptical — that because of the condition of the church they hadn't believed any kind of services could be taking place there. As I stood in the middle of the road, afraid they were just going to take him back, I could see the officer in the passenger side looking at me — my black dress and stockings and shoes — while the other one chuckled. "We're just going to get something to drink," he said. "We'll bring him right back."

We'd been told — when our request to have Joe there was approved — that we were not allowed to have any contact with him and that we'd have to stay back several feet from where he was. I didn't even look at him in the car. When the officers brought him back and parked near the entrance of the church's auxiliary building, Brett and I stood off to the side, away from the entrance. A few people had begun to arrive early, and I had to tell them they'd have to wait outside in the heat until the private viewing was over and Joe was gone.

When he emerged from the car, I saw that his ankles were shackled and his hands were cuffed behind his back. I hadn't seen him like that before, and I stood there trying not to register any emotion on my face as I watched him walk into the church, flanked by the two officers. In my memory, this happens in slow motion — like a trite scene from a movie — and I feel like I notice everything, particularly the sound of his feet shuffling in the leg restraints, the birds flying out of the sanctuary and settling in the tree across the street, the whoosh of the door as Mr. Croutch opens it to let them in.

When Joe is inside several feet, Brett and I follow, shutting the door behind us. The flowers haven't yet arrived, and the low-ceilinged room seems sparse, homely. Except for the pews they've managed to salvage and the folding chairs where the choir will sit, the room holds only an organ, a small podium and wooden chairs for the pastor and deacons, and the platform bearing the casket. Before Mr. Croutch shuts the doors to the makeshift sanctuary, I can see Joe standing before the open casket, his head bowed.

While Joe is inside, Aesha arrives with his daughter, PJ. Waiting with us, she explains to the child that she'll not be able to touch or speak to her father. When Joe comes out a short while later, his eyes are red, and I look at him a good long moment trying to make my face convey everything I am not allowed to say. Perhaps the officers are moved by all this — the grandson in restraints, the run-down church still wearing the vestiges of Katrina, the small congregation there to say goodbye to a woman who wanted nothing more than to come back home. Before the car pulls away, the officers roll down Joe's window to let him speak to us. Aesha and I — PJ between us — move a few tentative steps closer. "Love y'all," he says, and "I'm ok," before the car moves slowly down the street, toward the old, two-lane Highway 49.

During the home-going ceremony I can't help thinking of what recovery and rebuilding means in this little room dressed up to serve as the sanctuary. My grandmother had made the draperies that hung in the church, and she'd seen her own daughter eulogized before them. And yet here she was being remembered in a room that served as church cafeteria, beneath low ceiling tiles — warped and stained reminders that Katrina isn't over. As my niece PJ stood at the podium to remember her great-grandmother, I realized just how much she'd lost in this ordeal, and I imagined that for the rest of her life she'd remember this time as underscored by the devastation of Katrina. She could mark the passing of her great-grandmother, the arrest of her father — the turmoil of these years — as *aftermath*.

A week later, when Joe's letter arrives, I am relieved to hear from him, to have some words between us beyond the few he was able to say leaving the church.

He writes with the penmanship of a generation — younger than mine — who spent only a cursory amount of time practicing handwriting in school. Most of his letter is in small, neat print, only his name and valediction — *love* — written in cursive. In that way, everything he says seems to be disconnected, just as he is, from the life he left outside the prison — everything except what binds us: love and the talisman of our names. *We only have small, safe pens,* he explains, *so it's hard to write.* When he calls to ask if I have received the letter, he tells me that the facility is noisy and that he has to try to find quiet space to put his thoughts down on paper. He says he writes a draft and then copies a neater version to send to me. I imagine him on his bunk, or some corner he's found away from the noise and low-level chaos of day-to-day life, trying to write what he thinks I need to know, and I begin to wonder if there are things edited out of my letter.

Later, when we are able to speak on the phone, I hold back all the questions I have about the jail, waiting for him to fill in what he can, what he is comfortable telling. I am hoping for reassurance, for him to tell me that he is safe and that the place isn't so bad. But I keep thinking about his writing materials — that he used the word "safe" to describe what they are given, suggesting that there are other objects that are unsafe, that might be put to dangerous purposes. I try to keep my voice steady when we talk, to hide that I am afraid. I keep thinking that this is best for his state of mind, but I know better. I am keeping a silence to protect myself from knowing. So often this is what the silences — in families as well as in the public discourse of difficult events — are all about: if something isn't spoken, it isn't fully known, and we can absolve ourselves of the responsibility that knowing entails. And yet our civic duty as citizens requires that we not turn away from knowing and that we use what we know to continue working for the best society we can hope to achieve. In the ongoing narrative of Katrina and the aftermath, this means uncovering the difficult stories about the aftermath and "recovery" that are often suppressed. It means remembering both the natural disaster of the hurricane that hit the Mississippi Gulf Coast *as well as* the man-made disaster of the levee break in New Orleans — and the travesty of the early response to that break. It means reckoning with our own blindness and erasures affecting the national discourse of the largest natural disaster in our history.

Joe mentions very little of his situation in that first letter, and selfishly, I find it encouraging—if only because of what he doesn't say. Signing off, he tells me he's about to go play checkers, *maybe win some extra grits or something*—and I can go about my days trying to think of him playing a friendly game, banishing any idea that he might want or need more food. Over the course of several months, however, Joe's letters become more like personal meditations—things he writes to himself during those minutes he is able to find some private space. In that way, he begins a kind of recovery—a process of personal recovery—that is beyond the rebuilding of his life that will have to take place later. And as the trajectory of his letters changes, I learn more about the difficulties he faces every day. I see in his contemplation the incorporation of a new narrative, one that integrates his past with the uncertain future he faces—his story on a parallel track with the evolving story of memory, rebuilding, and recovery on the Mississippi Gulf Coast.

On August 28, 2008, I was being held in a facility in North Mississippi. The news reported that tropical storm Gustav destroyed parts of Jamaica, killing over sixty people. On August 30, 2008, one of the guards came into my area and shouted, "How many of y'all are from the coast? Gather round." I had a frightening feeling that this was about the storm. He told us that Hurricane Gustav was headed toward the coast—"So make sure you call your folks and say a prayer tonight."

This was a terrifying reminder of 2005. I began to worry about my daughter. I remember driving through town afterward with my grandmother as we left the shelter; it was like going through a maze, dodging the broken trees and fallen traffic lights. I could see the shock and disbelief on her face as she constantly asked, "How is the house?" While traveling we passed several people sitting in their cars on the side of the road, out of gas. There were no gas stations open, and traffic was backed up for miles. I saw families with their pets running alongside them as they pushed shopping carts with what little belongings they were able to save. It's been three years and I can still remember the frightened little girl I saw clinging to a dingy teddy bear that had clearly been through the storm.

In some areas of the coast you can still see abandoned buildings, boarded up and spray-painted with the words *We are here, We have a Gun, We will shoot*. These are reminders of the crimes committed and the actions people took to protect their homes. Burglaries and looting became major problems. Police issued warnings that if anyone was caught committing these crimes, they would receive a mandatory five-year jail sentence. Thieves would prey on houses hoping that they were empty from people evacuating before the storm — businesses as well. Business owners began opening their stores and handing out items. I saw a local store owner crying, saying, "If we don't give it to them, they will just take it." Police started allowing people take things from the stores as long as it was for survival — like food and water.

Through the mass of the crowd it was hard to tell who was taking things out of desperation and who out of ignorance. When I asked some of the people in my neighborhood what it was like for them — *how did you survive?* — they said:

"Man, the people here would be ok, we know how to survive under stressful times." "We are used to making the best of what little we have. Joe, you know that." And, "It's the upper-class people who panicked most under these conditions. Besides, the Bible warned us that this was gonna happen."

~~~

In the county jail, I talk to a guy who tells me he is awaiting trial. He's here for fraud. The house he lived in all his life was destroyed by Hurricane Katrina while he was incarcerated. And when he was released, he received a disaster check for about $12,000. He is in jail now because he wasn't *in* the house during the storm.

~~~

I talked to another guy who was incarcerated on the coast during Katrina. He told me how they had to use the bathroom in garbage bags and store them for a couple of weeks while wondering about the fate of their families. "With no TV and no telephones," he said, "that couple of weeks seemed like forever."

~~~

In the weeks stretching to months that my brother is in prison, Aesha and I talk on the phone and e-mail each other frequently. We are both anxious to know how he is doing, and so we tell each other anytime we get word from him in a letter or by phone. Months after the threat of Gustav out in the Gulf has passed, Aesha tells me something my brother has insisted she keep from me. At the county jail where he spent months awaiting sentencing, the mechanical system that controls the locking mechanism on the inmates' cell doors was broken. Each night at lockdown the guards padlocked the men into their cells. Had a need to evacuate the prisoners arisen — perhaps because of fire or a hurricane bringing floodwaters — it would not have been a speedy process. Each padlock would had to have been opened by hand, with a key.

When Joe and I next speak on the phone, I don't tell him what I have learned. We keep a fiction between us rooted in silence. I learn to weigh what he is telling me against what I know he must not be. Not until much later do I come to see that my silence was the heaviest.

~~~~

My first day in jail I'm immediately asked, "What you is?" — meaning *what gang are you in?* I quickly respond I'm just me. Most new inmates become affiliated and join organizations in order to ensure protection. Younger inmates, hoping to excel in gaining respect, often follow orders given by veteran inmates with higher rank. These young inmates are sometimes referred to as crash dummies.

Most arguments or verbal disagreements are followed by popular phrases such as "I'm not an inmate, I'm a convict" or "This ain't my first rodeo." I wonder why this is used as a form of bragging rights — or why respect is given for repeat visits to the penitentiary. Why not aim at other accomplishments to be proud of, or other ways to gain respect? Another phrase often repeated in prison is "Time does itself."

While lying on my bunk, I look around at the different men in the facility and ask myself what am I doing here?

How did this happen? I listen to the hopeless conversations, and I realize how lucky I am to have such a wonderful family who loves and supports me.

~~~~

One of my most pleasant childhood memories would have to be my first day of elementary school. This was the only year my sister and I attended the same school before she started high school. I was really excited about this day; I remember polishing my new loafers that I had stuffed with quarters instead of pennies. I wore slacks and a button-down shirt with my father's brown tie that my mother altered downstairs in her sewing room. I never told my sister how excited I was about that day.

Most of my childhood was normal — or so I thought. Things in our home seemed ok. I was a happy child; I had all of the things I wanted. With both parents at home, I thought my life was perfect. We lived in a big house in a nice neighborhood. There were many families on the street, so I had a lot of friends. It was the only neighborhood I had ever known, so it was nice to me. Prior to my imprisonment, I would drive by it, bringing back memories, trying to understand and put the pieces together.

~~~~

Reading my brother's words the first time, I wanted to believe only what was there, what I could see on the page. The narrative of me as part of that wonderful and supportive family suited my version of myself, and my willed blindness to other things, to what was unspoken and invisible, absolved me of more responsibility. In this way, I was not unlike those people content to look around certain areas of the post-Katrina landscape and praise the state for its remarkable recovery, while ignoring the dark underbelly reflected in the ongoing devastation of the lives of some of the poorest, least visible victims of the hurricane.

Reading them again, I am struck by what it means that he seems to be thinking out loud, not addressing his words to me but uttering them so that I might overhear: *I never told my sister how excited I was about that day; most of my childhood was normal; we lived in a big house in a nice neighborhood.* In all this time, I have never once written my brother a letter. I nearly tripped over furniture each time the phone rang so that I would not miss talking to him. I wired money through Western Union so that he could buy snacks and sodas at the prison canteen. I sent boxes of food and coffee and socks and books and music and underwear and aspirin and anything else he was allowed to ask for and receive. But it never occurred to me — and so I did not send — the one thing I know now he must have wanted more than anything: some words from me to hold on to longer than the ten minutes we were allowed to speak on the phone.

And in the midst of my silence, he begins on his own to recover some of what had been lost to him. He becomes the one of us most willing to voice what had not been said, giving more weight to what is spoken than to the silence I had been keeping — I thought to protect him — between us.

~~~~~

Growing up I really loved my father. We had a certain father-and-son bond. I remember we used to go for rides after dinner. We would listen to old soul music on his eight-track player, and he would let me take a few sips of his beer. I remember he bought himself some sort of hat with a feather in it. I liked it so much that he found a small one just like it to fit me.

I do recall one particular ride we took on the other side of town. I remember sitting on the porch talking to some woman with a short hairstyle. I think I was around eight years old. I later found out that she was the mother of my half brother. I only met him once at my grandfather's funeral.

~~~

The morning my mother and I left was very confusing to me. I don't remember going to sleep the night before, but I do remember leaving my house without saying goodbye to my father or my friends. I remember grabbing a few of my favorite things and leaving the rest behind, my mother explaining — trying to make me understand. I was very close to both of my parents, but I guess there is some sort of chemistry between a mother and child, and somehow I knew that I belonged with my mother. When we moved away from my father, my mother knew how much this had devastated me. She decided I needed counseling, so I started talking to Dr. Rocky. I had always been quiet and kept things to myself. But Dr. Rocky was an outlet: he tried to help me understand and realize that both my parents loved me. We talked about my father and some of the things he was going through and the reasons for some of his actions. We talked about domestic violence, something that I had no idea about — and I didn't know it was happening in our home. My mother was amazing — keeping a smile on her face, camouflaging her bruises with makeup, keeping me unaware of the abuse.

Some of these things are still difficult to talk about.

~~~

I never knew that my father had the kind of problems he had. He never showed them, or maybe I was too young to notice them. He never punished me, I can remember asking him for things or asking to go places and he would say go ask your mother, if she said no, like any other kid, I would be upset with her, now I realize that was his cowardly way of not having to tell me no, I haven't talked to my father for over twenty years, for some reason people find that hard to believe.

Facsimile reproduction of one of Joe's letters from prison, circa October 2008

Early in my childhood, my grandmother and I had a wonderful relationship. I would get so excited about going to visit her. I remember that I would call it "Sicky" because I couldn't pronounce Mississippi. Moving to Mississippi to live with her was very hard for me. It was a major change from living in Atlanta with my family. My grandmother was a wonderful lady, and she did the best she could, but raising a child who looked exactly like the man who murdered her only child had to be painful. I learned a lot from her. She taught me the importance of family, especially during the holidays. This will be my first Christmas without her and also my first Christmas incarcerated.

To all of this I respond with a 12×12-inch box of supplies:

Aftershave, unscented, in a plastic container
Tuna in pouches, not cans
Dental floss
Two tins of potato chips
Dried soup
Instant coffee, flavored
Solid deodorant
Lip balm
Any kind of candy in 16-ounce packaging
Small electric shaver
Cotton work gloves
Thermal plastic cup
Something to read
Boot insoles, size 9

December 9, 2008

Tonight I arrive at my new location: Pearl, Mississippi, approximately 120 miles from the last facility. A different town but basically the same building — four walls attached to a timeless revolving door. Inside these walls there's a different world entirely, a world that consists of its own unwritten laws and rules, a world filled with all sorts of personalities and custody levels. It seems like the bigger the crime you commit, or the larger the amount of drugs you were caught with, the more respect you have.

Almost everyone has a prison name, like *Really Real, Walt Luv, Anthea, Bun B, Hot Boy,* and *Pistol.* They call me *Coca Leaf* or *Joe Coca Leaf.* I realize that in the world of rehabilitation these may not sound like positive things, but when it comes to prison survival, respect is one of your greatest possessions.

~~~~

Sometimes a place like this can bring out the worst in you. When you're surrounded by negativity, it's very easy to lose focus. This place is filled with a variety of people. We spend a lot of time discussing our plans for the future. I look forward to starting over and living a new life. The fact that I don't plan on doing the things that got me here separates me from the people who don't plan on getting caught.

This is not my life.

~~~~

December 20, 2008

Today we had a shakedown. K-9 entered our zone, six or seven oversized country boys with attitudes in search of

marijuana, cell phones, and handmade weapons. They sel-
dom find them though. When you're confined to an area for
twenty-four hours a day, you get to know it — and its hiding
places — pretty well, better than anyone else, including the
dogs that sniff your surroundings while you're facedown on
the cold floor. From the corner of my eye I sneak a peek just
to catch a glimpse of the faces behind the yelling and cursing.

~~~~~

December 31, 2008

I'm preparing to enter a new year. It's not quite what I expected to be doing on this day, sitting around drinking "sexy
babies" — a popular drink throughout the prison system. It's
made of hot coffee, milk, coco, lots of sugar, and a Snick-
ers bar if you're lucky. This is our brew, or cocktail, and we
drink them one after the other like shots of liqueur at a bar as
we say goodbye to 2008, imagining what we would be doing
if we were out, hoping that 2009 will be a better year.

~~~~~

I am now located in a small town called Lucedale. I'm part
of a work program, and I work for the highway department.
I walk eight miles a day doing roadwork — free labor for
the state of Mississippi. I look at it as exercise; this is what I
constantly tell myself. This is how I preserve my pride, my
dignity. I begin my day by marking my calendar, grabbing
my work boots and safety jacket — bright orange with reflec-
tors — though I am not really concerned with safety, only
trying to hide my shirt with the words INMATE WORKER on
the back of it. Cars pass by: some people in them blow, some

wave, and some just stare. I wonder what they think when they see me: criminal, or just a human being who simply wants to pay his debt to society.

~~~~

Cycle
I am named after
my father; he's named after
his. No disrespect

to my grandfather —
resting — I pronounce my name
Jo-el instead of

Joel. I am nothing
like him. Although I am in
prison, I'm not him.

~~~~

January 12, 2009

Several months have passed, and I have learned to make the best of my situation and work with whatever I have — adjusting to things like hand washing my clothes in the sink and boiling my bottled water to make coffee instead of drinking warm water out of the sink as is expected. Some inmates draw tattoos or pictures for money or snacks from the prison store. These adaptations are often referred to as "convicting," but I don't like that term. What about creativity or ingenuity? We figured out a way to light a cigarette with a paperclip and an electrical socket, boil water with a hot wire and a piece of metal, and cut our hair with a comb and razor just to look presentable when our families come to visit.

If only we had utilized these talents in the free world.

~~~~~

A new inmate walks in. I've known him since high school. As soon as we make eye contact, without saying hello, he mumbles, "Man I can't believe I'm seeing you in a place like this." This reaction is all too familiar. It used to bother me a little bit. Now I think it sort of inspires me: if I stand out in this crowd, maybe I don't belong here.

Redux

SOME THINGS HAVE STAYED with me through all of this and happen in my memory as if they are still occurring — like a story I am rewriting until I get the ending right. I know too that it's a form of rebuilding.

The day of my brother's sentencing, July 14, 2008, is typical for south Mississippi — almost unbearably hot, the air thick with humidity. On the way to the courthouse, I notice a group of convicts in green- and white-striped pants working along the road — picking up trash, mowing the tall grass. Others are helping to spread tar over a patch of Highway 49, and the acrid smell comes through the car's air vents before we can close them. I read the letters on the prisoners' backs, MDOC — Mississippi Department of Corrections — and the words INMATE WORKER, an image of the contemporary chain gang.

Brett and I arrive at the courthouse, both of us in suits, just before 9:00 a.m. At the security checkpoint I empty my bag and watch the guard sift through the contents, embarrassed that I had not jettisoned more before coming. Aesha meets us on the other side, and we walk into the courtroom together and find seats a few rows back from the short barrier that divides the area where the attorneys sit from the rest of us. In a whisper she tells us that Joe's attorney can't be there this morning, that he's had some family emergency. Neither of us thinks this bodes well for the outcome, but we say nothing — afraid to put our worry into words.

When the judge enters — the Honorable Lisa Dodson — we watch her face and gestures for signs of her mood. After months of coming to these hearings, we know to try to surmise from her rulings on the cases of other defendants how she might respond when Joe stands before her. On several occasions, Joe's lawyer has asked for a postponement when he's thought she wasn't in her most charitable mood. He also made sure this is the judge who hears my brother's case — she's known for being thoughtful, empathetic. She knows Aesha too — from the days when Aesha worked as a clerk in the courtroom.

This morning, like many others, the cases she rules on have some link to Hurricane Katrina or the aftermath. A man accused of molesting the teenage daughter of a friend is pleading his case and answering her questions. Already a convicted sex offender, he is also being sentenced for not notifying the local authorities of his relocation to the area. He had come here from Florida with his backhoe to help clean up the friend's property and rebuild the house on it. When the judge asks why he didn't register as a sex offender when he moved here, he tells her the move was only *temporary*, that he was only "here because of the storm." Then he adds, "Anyway, I figure you people always know where I am." There's a spill of laughter in the room before we regain our composure, hoping we haven't angered the judge into handing down harsher sentences for our loved ones. She seems sympathetic when the friend stands up to give testimony on behalf of the accused. He asks for leniency because the man had been his friend, had helped him out after the hurricane. The daughter isn't in the courtroom, and I wonder what she would think about her father's request.

I am trembling by the time Joe stands before her, and the sentencing seems to take forever. Except for the funeral, this is the first time I've seem him since the hearing in which she ordered him into custody, nearly three weeks ago, and he is wearing the orange uniform given to inmates in the county jail instead of his street clothes. Somehow, he looks smaller in it, and the way the shirt hangs on his shoulders makes him appear hunched over and anxious despite his outward calm. Leaning forward, I strain to hear his words — but he is soft spoken, and his back is to us. I can't see his face when she delivers the sentence: fifteen years, six suspended. This is not what we'd hoped to hear, and all of us are doing the math in our heads: with nine years left to serve, he'll have to spend at least three years in prison. That's the least amount of time he'd have to do before being eligible for parole. In a letter to the judge, Brett and I had pledged to be part of his recovery effort, to help him get the rental units rebuilt and pay the delinquent taxes and assessments the city imposed for demolishing the blighted structures that remained after the storm. Hearing the sentence, we know a while will pass before Joe can begin rebuilding his life. On the coast, recovery takes a long time.

The deputies move swiftly once a sentence is recorded, and they immediately flank Joe to lead him out of the courtroom. I am biting the inside of my cheek to keep from tearing up so that he won't see me cry. But then, he never turns to look back — he goes through the same door he came out of, raising his hand for us only when he's nearly out of sight.

Stunned, the three of us leave the courtroom then, standing up as they call for the next defendant, and we don't stop until we pass security and reach the back door to the parking lot. Outside I stand in the sun wiping my eyes as Aesha and Brett hug each other and say goodbye. Then I hug her too, and Brett and I watch her get into her car so that we can stand there waving before heading to the airport. I wait until she is gone before I turn to Brett and ask — as I had when I first learned my brother was facing jail time — *how am I going to live when my heart is in prison?*

I recall that before we left that morning, Brett and I stood for a while next to the rental car with the doors open, waiting for the heat inside to dissipate. I was still wiping my face when a car pulled up beside us and a teenaged boy in the passenger side leaned out the window, asking for directions. "Can you help us?" he said. "We need to find the public library." He was riding with a woman who must have been his mother, and when she smiled at us, I could see that she was missing several of her front teeth. I remember too that the car had a Florida license plate — Escambia County — and that it was weighed down, the bumper nearly dragging the pavement. The back seat was loaded with what seemed to be all their possessions: I could see garbage bags spilling clothes, a couple of pillows and a comforter, the legs of an upended chair. With the windows rolled down, they were still sweating in the late morning heat, and I could imagine many reasons, beyond books, that they might need to reach the library: Internet access, an air-conditioned respite, a public restroom in a clean, comfortable building.

Turning to answer them, I felt an initial sense of relief that comes from being able to help — being able to answer a question or provide needed information to a stranger. The simplest of human interactions, like a greeting, it can change the course of a day. Nodding, I turned in the direction of the beach to point them toward it, raising my hand before I caught myself.

The downtown branch of the Gulfport public library was only a few blocks away, and for a moment I stood there, my hand in the air — a gesture like the beginning of a benediction — before I could think of what to say. All the clichés come to me now: *a stone's throw away, as the crow flies*, and — finally — *you can't get there from here*; the library had been destroyed by Hurricane Katrina. Even now, as I write, it hasn't been rebuilt.

I recall little else of that day — not the drive to the airport or our short flight back to Atlanta, nor what we did the rest of the evening. Mostly I see the way my brother raised his hand, leaving the courtroom, his back to us — a slight movement, not unlike the fulfillment of my own stalled gesture — as if he were pointing to a destination, some place not far up the road.

Natasha and Joe, Greenwood Mississippi, June 2007

Benediction

I thought that when I saw my brother
walking through the gates of the prison,
he would look like a man entering

his life. And he did. He carried
a small bag, holding it away from his body
as if he would not touch it, or

that it weighed almost nothing.
The clothes he wore seemed to belong
to someone else, like hand-me-downs

given a child who will one day
grow into them. Behind him, at the fence,
the inmates were waving, someone saying

All right now. And then,
my brother was walking toward us,
a few awkward steps at first until

he got it — how to hold up the too-big pants
with one hand, and in the other
carry everything else he had.

Joe and Aesha, September 2014.
Photograph by Glen Weisberger.

Epilogue

A few years ago, on one of my many journeys home to the Mississippi Gulf Coast, I saw on the side of the road a politician's campaign placard: "Katrina isn't over," the sign read. I could see then, as I can now — ten years after the hurricane — that it is true.

While Joe was in prison, our grandmother's house stayed boarded up, and another kind of devastation began to overtake it: from the inside, termites eating through the floor, the roof falling in on itself; from the outside, nothing more dramatic than rain and our absence and the passage of time. This is true of many of the houses people have not been able to repair, and one by one they've been torn down as the city's leaders endeavor to erase the blight — so much of it still in our old neighborhood.

Joe's fight to keep our grandmother's house from demolition meant that he'd mow the grass weekly, cut back the encroaching brush, and clear the lot of debris. A blue hydrangea had grown beside the front steps as long as I can remember, and Joe would prune it regularly to keep it blooming. This is just one way that he attempted to hold onto some part of the past, something that could anchor us to a time before Hurricane Katrina. My grandmother had planted the seeds, had watered and nurtured the shrub all those years with her own hands. It wasn't long before the sign Joe was dreading, CONDEMNED, emblazoned the front door. He called to tell me the house would have to come down.

Years ago, around the same time I wrote the words *Natural*

Disaster in my notebook, I also began writing a poem called "Permanence" — a meditation on the opposite of that notion. Already I was beginning to imagine a time in which the things that held traces of us, my family's imprint on the landscape, would be erased. The house had stood on land we'd owned for more than a hundred years, a landmark of the history of several generations. It would be gone in an afternoon.

The city's mandate to demolish the house came at the same time that Joe completed his sentence and was no longer bound by parole or probation. He was free to begin his life again; he could even leave Mississippi for good. Taking down the house would be the last task he had to do before moving on. Before the start of hurricane season last year, Joe hired a couple of guys he knew, a bulldozer, and a large dumpster to haul everything away.

During the demolition Joe texted me photographs of the machine razing everything left on the land, including the hydrangea. In one picture, the house's left side had been torn off, and I could look into the room that had been my bedroom as if looking into the open side of a discarded dollhouse — an imitation, small and inhabitable. Not being there was like missing a wake, and Joe told me the years washed over him as he stood watching. It was a break with his past. When he walked away, all that remained was the vacant lot and dirt turned over as if for a burial.

Last September, Joe and Aesha married in an intimate ceremony on a sun-swept beach. As I write this, they are searching for a new home here in the Atlanta area. Joe was born here, and he's been waiting most of his life — since our mother was killed — to make his way back. I've not been back to Gulfport since before the demolition, and so in my mind's eye, hunkered there against forgetting, the house still stands, not as in recent years, but intact — as it was when I was growing up. When I think of the reality of what's happened I imagine, too, that occasionally someone must give directions, pointing toward vanished landmarks in North Gulfport: *If you pass the lot where Mrs. Turnbough used to live you've gone too far.*

With all the rebuilding now taking place along the beach and in historic communities, it is hard to know what narrative is being inscribed onto the landscape of the Gulf Coast — only that something has been set in motion that we'll not be able to see clearly until we are far beyond it. Hegel wrote: "The owl of Minerva flies only at dusk," suggesting that the wisdom of an era arises only at the end of it.

We've come far from those early days of loss and devastation, in the immediate aftermath of the storm, and yet, for Joe and many people like him, Katrina might never completely be over. Parts of it stay with us — our grief, our many losses. The felony conviction stays with Joe, haunting his ability to find work with some employers who look only at the checked box and not at the person who has redeemed his life. Still, he continues to rebuild: he's taken courses at a community college, earned a certificate in welding, and secured a job as head of the plumbing department in a hardware store — each another step toward putting the past farther behind him. Perhaps this is the most we can hope for: that as the memory of the hurricane fades into the background of our collective imagination, the worst experiences of it receding into the distance, Katrina may become, like Hurricane Camille before it, a cautionary tale and marker of time — a way to link the narratives of our past to our ever-evolving future: *Before* and *After*.

Acknowledgments

There are many people to whom I owe a great deal of thanks: Ted Genoways, editor of the *Virginia Quarterly Review*, without whose ideas and encouragement this book would never have been written; Erika Stevens, editor at the University of Georgia Press, whose vision, compassion, and empathy guided me through to the final word; my agent, Rob McQuilkin, whose advice is always just right; Aesha Qawiy, Tamara Jones, Susan Glisson, Tayari Jones, and D. Allen Mitchell — a congregation of supporters whose knowledge and generosity kept me going and who were always willing to talk through anything I asked; all the folks in Mississippi, some named in these pages and some not, who answered graciously my many questions; my husband, Brett, whose ongoing support is immeasurable; and finally, my brother Joe — whose story was always *the* story.

Thanks also to the *Virginia Quarterly Review*, in whose pages some of this work first appeared, and to Professor Talbot Brewer and the Page-Barbour Lecture Series at the University of Virginia where, in 2007, I presented some sections of this book.

Printed in the USA
CPSIA information can be obtained
at www.ICGtesting.com
LVHW031245140124
768958LV00006B/381

9 780820 349022